D0215076

These the Companions

These the Companions
Recollections

Donald Davie

Cambridge University Press
Cambridge
London   New York   New Rochelle
Melbourne   Sydney

Published by the Press Syndicate of the University of Cambridge
The Pitt Building, Trumpington Street, Cambridge CB2 1RP
32 East 57th Street, New York, NY 10022, USA
296 Beaconsfield Parade, Middle Park, Melbourne 3206, Australia

© Cambridge University Press 1982

First published 1982

Printed in Great Britain at the University Press, Cambridge

Library of Contress catalogue card number: 81–17098

British Library Cataloguing in Publication Data
Davie, Donald
These the companions.
1. Davie, Donald   2. Authors, English – 20th century
– Biography
I. Title
820'.9   PR6007.A667
ISBN 0-521-24511-7

Contents

Illustrations

(*mostly by Doreen Davie*)

To the grandsons
Peter, Jonathan, and Joseph Davie
and Christopher McKay

Acknowledgments

A small part of Chapter 1 of what follows appeared originally in the New York miscellany *Prose*, and was reprinted in *Trying to Explain* (University of Michigan Press, and Carcanet Press). Sections of Chapter 2 and Chapter 6 appeared in *My Cambridge*, edited by Ronald Hayman. And in a different form Chapter 11 was printed in *The Sewanee Review*. I am grateful to these editors and publishers for their courtesy.

D.D.

Lordly men are to earth o'ergiven
　　these the companions:
Fordie that wrote of giants
　　and William who dreamed of nobility
　　and Jim the comedian singing:
　　　　"Blarney castle me darlin'
　　　　you're nothing now but a STOWne"
and Plarr talking of mathematics
　　or Jepson lover of jade

　　　　　　　(Ezra Pound, *The Pisan Cantos*)

Foreword

Sometimes I think I have lived for ever, or nearly. This happens when I hear or read people talking of 'the Fifties', meaning the 1950s, as if that period were as distant in history as the 1850s or the 1650s. It happens when I realize that the journalists now influential, whether in Britain or the U.S., or for that matter in France, are young enough for a date like 1968 to seem to them, in all seriousness and all sincerity, a momentous turning-point not just for them but for anyone who wants to understand these times we are living in. It happens when I realize that for my own sons, now grown up, Orde Wingate is a name as legendary as Oliver Cromwell. At such times I feel an enormous responsibility: how much that I have experienced, little as any of it reached the headlines, will swirl away into oblivion unless I get it down on paper, since no one else seems inclined to try! But just as often, and indeed almost automatically as the ebb succeeds the flood, I find myself with nothing to say: or with nothing to say that I have not said already, obliquely in poems, or inconsiderately in interviews, or implicitly in what I have written that looks like literary criticism or literary history. Who is it one is writing for? Who cares anyway? And why should they? A sort of paralysis comes.

A simple straightforward chronicle – in 1959 I was doing this, in 1960 I seem to have been doing that – will always have value, so long as people have any interest in the historical record of past times. But on the one hand we cannot any longer, it seems to me, take that interest for granted. And in any case the chronicler, the humble annalist, is one sort of creature; the historian is another, with more presumption. If I find that I want to risk the more presumptuous way, I tell myself that I am presumptuous not for myself but on behalf of that faculty, the imagination, which the historian may or must employ, though the chronicler may not. How to recollect in the imagination a past that all the same shall not be imaginary . . .? With a programme like that, no one can be surprised if what blocks him is a paucity of material, not any unmanageable abundance. One remembers this or that; but to recollect it in the imagination so as to *re-create* it – ah, faced with that requirement one finds the usable, the remarkable past, quite suddenly and drastically contracted. How much of life one has lived, how many people and occasions one has encountered, without the imagination being stirred in any way at all! The chronicler need not worry about this, but the historian must, much to his dismay. What he has to guard against, in the midst of his discourage-ment, is the temptation to re-admit the chronicler in an immodest dis-guise, as the categorizer or (as we now have it) 'the analyst'; one who, even as he records the past, sorts it out into structures of ideas that we have laxly agreed to regard as important for the passing moment. Two examples: 'angry young men', and 'grammar-school boys' – two formulae that have at the present day the peculiar fustiness that attaches to the bright ideas of yesterday. My path through life may be thought to illus-trate both these formulae: and insofar as such formulae have truth (for undoubtedly they have some), I do not repudiate them. But how little of truth they have, or how little that the imagination can profit by! Is it not their function indeed precisely to exclude or discount the reports of the imagination, which must always stammer, in the face of them, that it is concerned with one particular person, in one place, at one time, in one sort of weather?

To generalize, said William Blake, is to be an idiot. He might as well have said that it is to be human. For no annalist, however self-effacing, can escape generalizing by implication. It is not true that simply choosing what to record implies generalizing; for one may choose, as I have tried to do, to record only such particulars as stir one's imagination and one's affections. But a simple record of episodes and personalities, one after another, is intolerable. Part of the record is precisely the reflections that the particular episode or character stirs one to. And so such reflections, which must be of the nature of generalizations, are part of the imaginative record. But what the imagination demands is that the occurrence or the person be rendered with a fullness that invites different reflections from those of the narrator. And so, in what I am to write, I shall try to remember that the representation counts for far more than whatever inferences I may be tempted to draw from it.

It should be said that I have known, or at least encountered, certain more or less famous people who do not figure in the pages that follow, where their places are taken by people who are, and in many cases will remain, obscure. If this should seem to prove that I am a democrat in these matters, I shall be happy.

If I could tell myself that what I have to say is *representative*, I should be more confident than I am about what appeal and interest it has, and to whom. If I could subtitle the book 'a writer's recollections', or 'a poet's', 'a critic's' or 'a teacher's', then my readers might have a better idea what to expect. But however it may have been in the past, I cannot now honestly see myself as representative in any of these categories. I have been all of these things, and have tried not to be amateurish about any of them; but it's impossible to single out any one of them and declare that one to be my profession, or my vocation. 'Writer' is the one I like best, because it's the most capacious. But I am not, and have never wanted to be, 'writer' in the single-minded and consuming sense in which a Virginia Woolf and an Ernest Hemingway could subscribe themselves 'writers'. Does this mean that I have wobbled and havered, eking out my incapacities in any one *role* by switching back and forth between that one and others? Or does it point to one general incapacity – for *dedication*? The questions do not worry me, and they need not worry the reader. For certainly I'm not writing to vindicate myself, if only because in this book I am not the principal character. You must bear with the first person singular only so as to have me introduce you to persons and places and ambiences that have a singularity and a value such as I won't claim for myself.

Donald Davie
Nashville, Tennessee, 1980

1

A West Riding boyhood

In California, one summer afternoon in 1971, soon after my 49th birthday, I slept and had a dream. I dreamed that I was walking with my father, who is dead, and my older son, who is now a father himself but in the dream was a child. I remember thinking, in the dream itself or else at the moment of waking, that a collier would speak of him as 'my little lad'. And in the dream we were among the collieries, in the South Yorkshire of my boyhood. Rawmarsh was the name that came into my head, and certainly Rawmarsh is a place in that neighbourhood, though I'm not sure that I've ever been there. As the dream began I decided suddenly that I was 'going home', and I plunged away from my dad and my little lad, rushing and sliding on my own through a scene that is common enough in those parts – old pithills or slagheaps, tilted steeply one against another, quite bare and sterile, with a narrow defile between them. The sun was blazing, it was very hot, and I knew it was Sunday morning. The spoil, the slag, was not grey-black but reddish, as it can be sometimes. And on I pelted, on and down, the red slopes getting steeper each side of me, and the path between them, beaten hard, getting more straitened. I came to a faint fork and careered, without deliberation, to the left. And then I stopped, suddenly assailed with a sort of horror – at the heat, the redness all round, the emptiness, and being alone. It impressed me of a sudden that I had come the wrong way, so I turned, rushed back uphill, and took the other arm of the fork. And yet, oddly, as I swung around I seemed to see from the tail of my eye that a gable-end showed itself down the narrow pass I was turning from, and not so far down either. But that was as might be, I thought; for the other fork soon brought me among houses which it seemed that I knew and could name as Darfield – an actual village, and one that I know well enough, though not the precise scene that my dream presented to me. A collier, in choking collar and stiff suit for Sunday, came walking there with his 'little lad'. And as I approached them the boy said something that I could not catch, though it must have been a plea for ice-cream. For the father answered, not unkindly, 'Ice-cream? Theer's thi ice-cream,' pointing to the flagstones black and cool in the shadows of the shuttered houses. The place was a spacious yard – in the Yorkshire sense of the word, not the American – at a street's end, with houses round it on three sides, or maybe only on two. 'Come in here,' the collier said to me; and the sun came in there, hot again, in a bare shop that he must have unlocked, there on the un-shadowed side of the square. He leaned on the counter, a telephone to his ear, while I waited, saying, 'I don't need the 'bus. Just show me the road to Barnsley. I'm going to walk.' He was a big strong fellow, and though he had doffed his jacket the sweat was streaking his red arms from under the rolled-up sleeves of his red-striped shirt. But I didn't care any more; it couldn't be far to Barnsley. And in any case I was safe with him.

Like any dream, this one can be construed. But I suspect a dream yields instruction only if we duck around the allegories which it seems to promise, and come into the shafts of light which it throws out obliquely. And thus the first thing that I'm made to realize about myself, with this dream in mind, is how constantly, throughout my boyhood but also ever since, my strongest and most common emotion has been fear. Fear, or else perhaps apprehension; for the fear has not been of any one thing or person, not even of any definable happening, but always unlocalized, unfocused, pervasive. I have been a coward before life; always, against the run of the evidence, I have expected the worst. What I mean is only, less flamboyantly, that I am a great 'worrier'; can always find something to worry about. Reading John Masefield's *So Long to Learn*, I notice how his childhood was also hedged about with fears, but with fears that could be named – bulls, hornets, adders, the gypsies; and how each of these fears, sharpened and inculcated by the prohibitions or warnings of grown-ups, had a sort of twisted reason to it, either in the actual conditions of nineteenth-century rural England or in past conditions still preserved in the folk memory. My fears were not of that kind; they were always of the unknown, as now they are of the unforeseeable. My parents were not only kind, but also enlightened; they were sure that only cruel or unenlightened parents peopled a child's world with bogies. It was not they who fed my fears. No one fed them. They throve on a spectral diet, and might even have shrunk a little if they had had something corporeal to bite on.

The only material fear that I can remember is of 'rough boys', who were to be recognized in Barnsley about 1930 because they wore jerseys (and also, the roughest of them, wooden clogs), whereas gentle or gentle-manly or nice boys wore blouses, as I did. But this was not a serious fear, and did not survive the day when my worst tormentor turned out to wear a blouse and to be shod in sandals. Barnsley society, as it was known to a schoolboy, was rigorously simplified and, as I see now, truncated: there were only two classes – proletariat and petty bourgeois. Solicitors, cler-gymen, doctors (though not dentists) sent their children away to board-ing-schools; and so, effectively, in St Mary's School there were only the sons of colliers and the sons of small shopkeepers like my father. (It comes to me now that the sons of artisans, of carpenters for instance, were classified sartorially, as jersey-wearers or blouse-wearers; we had our own sumptuary laws, though they were flexible.) Barnsley was a society so overwhelmingly proletarian that it always was, as it still is, an impregnable Labour stronghold in both municipal and national politics. We always voted the other ticket, without hope. And at times I have indulged the notion that, growing up thus in a disfranchised minority, and learning at my mother's knee the inevitable tension between us the few and them the many, I was conditioned to a political attitude that used to be called *poujadiste*; and I have fancied that I detected in myself the sentiments of a petty bourgeois Fascist. My dream is welcome to me because it disproves that. Perhaps it even disproves the Marxist theory of classes. For in the dream my Samaritan was undeniably proletarian, beneficent and to be trusted, a protector.

It would be odd if it were otherwise. For my mother was herself born in a colliery cottage; and though my maternal grandfather John Sugden ended his days (rheumatically and before I was born) as a colliery under-manager, he must have begun – I now realize – at the pit-face. I had an uncle who was a joiner, and another who was a seaman in Liverpool. So too my grandfather Davie had come north out of Dorset as a signalman with the railway. And both my grandmothers had been domestic servants. To be sure they had all 'bettered themselves', and though I don't remember that expression being used in my childhood, plainly the idea behind it was still potent in my parents' generation, and even indeed in my own. How ingrained it is in the English, and how tediously mean-minded, this game of class-distinctions! I'm ashamed to find it is a game that I still play myself, as these comments show.

The slagheap scenery of my dream is one that as a child I often walked through, most often with my father, and mostly on a Sunday. We lived on Dodworth Road, and I remember, out of many, two short walks in particular that led through slagheaps: one cut through between Dodworth and Higham, heading towards Hugsett woods and Silkstone; and the other went through Dodworth and past Gilroyd to Stainbrough. This second one, though it was longer, was better, because near Gilroyd it passed by a tunnel under a railway where one could sometimes see what was then the most powerful locomotive in England hauling coal-wagons up the gradient. And Stainbrough, when one got to it, was not a mining village but manorial, sparsely grouped at the gates of the great park round Stainbrough Hall. There were plenty of pockets like that, green and pastoral and manorial, among the industrial wastes. Indeed, if I were to measure the acreage of each kind, discounting for instance the fumes from the one that blew across the other, it would be

3

the industrialized acres that would count as the pockets. We, my brother and I, were very early educated to this sort of accountancy, measuring the greater attractiveness of one walk over another according as there was more of the one kind of landscape than of the other. And yet I think none of us – my mother and father no more than us children – truly experienced the slagheap scenery as ugly, a privation, an image of sterility. Thus, although the red landscapes of my dream plead to be construed as infernal, I distrust the allegory here also. Though my dreamed-of panic among them was sharp and frightening, I suspect that panic is what it was – a fear of the empty and the silently other, of the great god Pan, strange as that must seem. For I remember vividly the initiation-rite which I imposed on myself, at puberty I suppose; and it was a Sunday walk *on my own*, through Hugsett woods in fact, the unformed and nameless horrors crowding at me, just as they are supposed to do, from among the mossy boles. That, it seems to me, was the prefiguring of what I experienced in dreaming. Pan, I conclude, dwells for me as much in industrial landscapes as in sylvan ones. And panic in that strict sense is an experience that I know very well; I experience it still, as I did not many months before I dreamed my dream – it came to me then in Calaveras Big Trees, California.

About the slagheaps we were, I suppose, ambivalent. Certainly my mother was. In her it was very striking, and informed her feelings about the West Riding in general. She was fiercely loyal to the region, and too ready to see and resent slights upon the Riding in the talk of people we knew who lived in Barnsley but had been brought up elsewhere. And yet it was she, I think, who planted in me the conviction that my native landscape was a sort of aberration; that the norm which it distorted,

Barnsley on a summer evening

though it could be perceived in places like Stainbrough, was serenely and securely to be found only elsewhere, outside the West Riding altogether. The reason was, I now believe, that in the tiny very literary group of us, she was the most literary. For the truth was of course that in English literature one found many an image of Stainbrough, but none of Gilroyd or Darfield. This has changed. The poems and stories in Ted Hughes's *Crow* or his *Wodwo* take place in a scenery which is that of my dream; and in fact Ted Hughes was reared in just my neighbourhood. But thirty or forty years ago there were only Arnold Bennett and D. H. Lawrence – my mother read both these authors – to suggest, partially and uncertainly, that our industrially ravaged landscape was being assimilated and acknowledged by the English imagination. If English literature imparted wisdom and instruction, as we were sure it did, that wisdom could not be separated from the manorial or pastoral images in which, time and again, it had been conveyed.

On the other hand, if we were a very literary lot, we were not musical in the least. This fact, and the oddity of it, came home to me only long after, discovering how much music meant to most of the people I associated with, beginning with my wife. We always had an upright piano in the house, and made use of it. My father in particular, in a strained but serviceable baritone, sang pieces from old musical comedies like 'No, No, Nanette' and 'Our Miss Gibbs', as well as from Gilbert and Sullivan, and would accompany himself. Also, 'the sing-song' was an accepted domestic institution, particularly at festive times like Christmas but not only then; and when we entertained guests, but also when we were by ourselves. Then we would sing folk-songs like 'Barbara Allen' and art-songs like 'Drink to me only with thine eyes', 'By the Banks of Allan

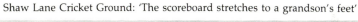

Shaw Lane Cricket Ground: 'The scoreboard stretches to a grandson's feet'

Victorian shop-front, Barnsley

Water and 'The Bells of Aberdovey': also – quite blithely jumping the
Atlantic without being aware of it – 'Riding down from Bangor/On an
eastern train', and 'Shenandoah' and 'Sewanee River'. (I remember
identifying Bangor as a town in North Wales, and puzzling mildly about
'weeks of hunting in the woods of Maine', finally deciding that Maine
must be an area I didn't know of, in or about Snowdonia or the Wirral.)
There were the Christmas carols, and 'Solomon Levi', and negro minstrel
songs, and 'Gaudeamus Igitur', and some of Tom Moore; in fact, the
full indiscriminate range represented by *The Scottish Students' Song Book*,
which I remember from my earliest days as a greatly cherished and much-
handled book that came first to hand when one lifted the seat of the piano-
stool. (My father, always a pushover for Scottish nostalgia, in his last years
took great pleasure from Andy Stewart, frank and upstanding and kilted
on the T.V., singing, 'There was a sojer, a Scottish sojer'; he bought the
music, and would play it and sing it, dear man.)

I loved these sessions, have loved them ever since, and love them
still; but have had to learn that I cannot be indulged in them at all often,
because it appears that, though my voice is powerful, I 'have no ear'. In
fact I could have learned this fact about myself quite early, when the
music master at Barnsley Grammar School (whose surname escapes me,
though his given names were John Thomas – an occasion for ribaldry)
stopped a chorus to ask 'Who is making that terrible noise?' to be answered resignedly by several class-mates: 'It's Davie, sir; he always
sings like that.' Moreover my parents sent me, as a little boy, to take
piano-lessons, which I pursued doggedly to the stage where I could take a
rudimentary examination; a few marks were allocated to an 'ear-test',
and my piano-teacher intimated gently that this was one part of the
examination I must just suffer through. So it proved; for the examiner
having struck a key that I was required to name, hearing me (who had no
option) say the first thing that came into my head, hammered away at the
key, expostulating 'C sharp, boy? *C sharp?*' Thus reduced almost to tears,
nevertheless I was in the event awarded an inglorious pass by the examiner – who was none other than the great Sir Richard Terry, whose
collections of sea-shanties and 'Salt-water Ballads' I have learned, in the
years since and out of what I must suppose to be my invincible ignorance,
to be grateful for. Despite this irrefutable evidence in my past, I yet as a
young man took such pleasure in hearing myself render shanties like 'The
Black Ball Line', or ballads like 'Admiral Benbow', that I could not believe
my renderings, approximate though they were, were excruciating to
others. Of late years, painfully persuaded of this, I have acquiesced in
the decision that I can be allowed to give voice only when I and those
around me are sufficiently drunk for the cacophony not to matter. (One

7

such happily drunken occasion was when, not many years ago, John Montague visited us in California, when the welkin, I suppose, rang, I suppose, with 'Charlie is my darling' and 'My Bonny lies over the ocean' and other Jacobite songs which, shouted more or less in concord by me and Montague, an Irish nationalist, afforded, I can't help thinking, a curious gloss on 'colonialism'.) I confess that, when I am alone in the house, I sometimes still permit myself a recital, solo and unaccompanied, which soon brings tears to my eyes.

Can I then, or can I not, declare myself remarkably unmusical? Should I not say rather, of myself and of my family (in which I was only the extreme case), that we were musical after our fashion, a fashion remarkably rudimentary and unsophisticated? The question matters to me because, however one takes it, there seems no doubt that I am musically a philistine. And sometimes I remember this uncomfortably, when I am in full derisive cry after the literary philistines who have repudiated or misrepresented the poetry that I admire. If the boot were on the other, the musical, foot, I should be in the pillory, and they would be justly fulminating and jeering. For it is true that I have seldom behaved so badly as when, gritting my teeth, I have accompanied my wife or some friends to an orchestral concert; except when I have been dragged along to that more excruciating boredom, *opera*! (And I have in mind Rossini's, Mozart's.) This means, though I do not remember it often enough, that I can sympathize not just with the obtuseness of the philistine, but with the angry hostility which that obtuseness engenders. It is all a put-down and a put-on, these pretensions of 'high' art! Having felt that myself, hearing my friends exultant over an opera performance that has reduced me to self-pitying bad temper, how can I be wholly unsympathetic when I detect the same bitterly aggrieved tone in what is said or written of the poetry of Basil Bunting, say, of Ezra Pound, even of Cowper or of Doctor Johnson? And indeed I believe that much needless suffering could be eliminated on all sides if we admitted that, just as there are people like me tone-deaf to music, so there are many more people than is usually acknowledged who are tone-deaf to poetry – or, to press the point home, to language in general as literature exploits it. Such people, through no fault of their own and however hard they try, will never understand what we professional fuglemen for literature are talking about, however much we hector them. And these people, who I suspect are numerous, have the right to be left alone. It is not after all true that one cannot be fully human unless one can distinguish Dryden's handling of the couplet from Pope's!

At all events, so I am now compelled to remember, my childhood not only endorsed in me my deafness to all the higher reaches of music but gave me, in case I had wanted to avail myself of the model, an instance of aggressive hostility towards them, those 'pretensions'. There comes before me the tall and lanky figure of the bank-clerk, Harold Rose, who lived opposite and would cross the road, some evenings, to play chess with my father. My mother, though I believe it was her acquaintance with Harold's wife, Beryl, that had initiated our relationship with 'the Roses', resented these visits by Harold; for she shared with the woman who was to be my mother-in-law a conviction of being ill-used whenever an outsider visited unannounced or without formal invitation. And she had reason to resent the Roses anyhow, because both Beryl and more particularly Harold had unguardedly reflected on the provincial grubbiness of Barnsley by the admittedly not very exalted standard of their own home town of Kettering, in the East Midlands. But what particularly incensed her, or else what she picked on as a specific grievance, was Harold Rose's enthusiasm for Tchaikovsky – an enthusiasm which, when we had visited the Roses, had provoked from him a sequence of thunderous chords on his own piano, and which, while my father pondered the next move on the chess-board, Harold would at times indulge with similar brief performances on our own instrument. 'Tchaikovsky' my mother would subsequently enunciate, with withering sarcastic emphasis, to the family circle; and cast her eyes to heaven. The name, I believe, was as novel to her and my father as to my brother and me; and I fear there was not lacking the supposedly self-evident implication that a worthwhile composer could not bear a name made up of such jawbreakingly Slavic syllables. (Was it not common knowledge that all the great composers – whose works however we were content to hear about, rather than hear – were Germans?) In justice to my mother it must be said however that her dislike of Tchaikovsky had some aesthetic substance: he was *loud*, he was over-emphatic, as certainly he was, when interpreted by Harold Rose. And I should not like to guess how much I owe, to this early experience of aesthetic judgment, my own proclivity to judge, in other arts than music, the loud as always *too* loud, the emphatic as *over*-emphatic.

This account does not begin to exhaust my worries about music and about philistinism. 'He that hath not music in his soul', says Shakespeare somewhere, and proceeds to predicate of such a creature the most lamentable consequences. I have taken note of that; and was only a little reassured when my Cambridge tutor, Tom Henn, expatiated half-seriously to the Shirley Society of St Catharine's College how it was normal for the poet to be tone-deaf, since his ear was for rhythm, and therefore could not afford to be distracted by considerations of tone and key. The prime instance of course – inevitably, since Henn was the speaker – was

Yeats, who is said to have known when the national anthem was played (whether British or Irish) only because people around him were getting up and standing to attention. That was gratifying to me, certainly; though I soon began to wonder if there were not cases that could be cited on the other side of the question. Milton, for instance; does not the evidence suggest that he was not much less responsive to music than to poetry? As for the musical philistine, such as I judge myself to be, does not his condition provoke very troublesome questions; in particular, whether in any art an instructed taste for the best does not drive out a capacity to respond to the halfway good, the respectably mediocre? Or again, if I had been able to respond at anything like the appropriately poignant level to Mozart and Beethoven, might not this have disabled my response to the artless melodies of folk-song, for instance as manipulated by Robert Burns? Does not a taste for the best inevitably emasculate a capacity to respond to the merely good? Transpose that question from music into literature, and (for me anyway) 'hark what discord follows'! Some of these disquiets and unanswerable conundrums I packed into a poem that I wrote in the 1960s, set as it happens in Italy, and called 'The Cypress Avenue':

My companion kept exclaiming
At fugitive aromas;
She was making a happy fuss
Of flower-naming.

And I, who had taken her there . . .
Not one scent could I name
In the resinous die-straight avenue's
Plume-irrigated air.

Her world was properly indexed:
The names were in my head
Familiar, double-columned, but
Hardly a page of text.

Just the swaying channel of shade;
The stippling everywhere
Of an otherwise dust-choked country;
The difference cypress made.

* * * * * * * * * * * *

That night at the family sing-song
She had no repertoire;
Her ear was a true one, though
Her voice not very strong.

10

And that was an index too!
Hymns, shanties, popular numbers,
Ballads, rounds – how many
It turned out that we knew!

And what an encyclopaedia
Of smudged ill-printed feeling
They opened up, although to
Only a coarsened ear.

The 'she' of this poem, 'my companion', is our old Dublin friend Helen Watson, who (bless her!) has never objected to, but rather embraced, the poem's making use of her in the way it does. And there are things in the poem – for instance, my ignorance of the gardener's practical knowledge of botany – which lay around in my head to be taken up and dealt with only many years later. But the poem at any rate – and not for the last time in these memoirs, I suspect, I find myself spelling out what a poem has already said succinctly – raises the question whether the philistine, in music or poetry or whatever else, has not access to legitimate pleasures which further education and refinement would only close to him.

The guileless egotism of a child that feels secure, its complacent confidence that the entire household revolves around itself and its siblings, can last for a very long time. I reflect with wry astonishment that only a very few years ago it seemed to me that my parents must have spent a lot of time competing, more or less consciously, for the affections of their children. Almost certainly they had better things to do. That I should think otherwise was a projection on to them of my own shifts in allegiance from one to the other. Until I was about fifteen, I was very close to my mother, thereafter closer to my father – which is, I dare say, a natural and proper progression for a male child. However, some of the time it felt very much like *siding* with one of them against the other. For my mother had an uncertain temper, and at times, there is no doubt of it, she *nagged*. And so at times I sympathized with my father, in a way that he presumably didn't recognize and probably wouldn't have liked. My mother, as a self-educated woman with a modest profession which she gave up in order to marry and raise a family, was subject to the cross-pressures of feeling, and the obscure sense of injustice, which the Women's Liberation Movement has recently done so much to bring into the open; and I see now, with sympathy for her, that it was this that lay behind much of her irritability.

As for my father, he was not austere, nor in the allegedly English way afraid of expressing his emotions and acknowledging them. Quite the contrary: as a young man he had deployed, and as an oldish man he recovered, notably histrionic talents which descend through me to his grandchildren. His emotions were easily stirred, by an imagined situation or by seeing himself in an imagined or halfway imagined role. The situations and roles were, for choice, comic; he was a mime, a clown, an impersonator, a wit. But the lachrymose and the pathetic he could respond to just as promptly, though he gave less play to these sides of himself. My mother found it more difficult than he did, to give her feelings unimpeded expression. And, if I know myself, I inherit from her a similar impediment. Hence, in my case and supposedly in hers also, one more reason for treasuring the bequest of literature; as a great battery or repertoire of masks and conventions, by and through which one may 'speak out' without seeming to. Accordingly I honour wistfully and fiercely those poets who can speak frankly to their fellows, who if they have piety towards the inherited past and its idioms, have different motives for that from the ones I detect in myself; my fellow-feeling, however, goes out to those artists – Thomas Hardy certainly, T. S. Eliot less directly – who are devoted to past styles as to a way of saying and yet not saying, laying bare and yet covering up, confessional and reticent at once. And yet, clearly, in order to make such poems for myself, I needed just those histrionic and play-acting capacities that were in my father's gift rather than my mother's. In my thirties, when I was still the Cambridge purist inordinately suspicious of the stagey, I was still my mother's son; but over the years since, I have come to trust, and to delight in, the inventive caprice of the comedian that my father was.

His gregarious good humour, his liveliness and waggishness, are not qualities that one readily associates with the deacon of a Baptist chapel. And yet he was not an anomaly, not 'out of his element'. He was genuinely a religious man, though diffident and constrained about the devotional side of 'chapel', to just the extent that he was exuberant in and about its social side. For his gifts as a mimic and a joker were not shown only in his family life, where they sparkled for his children and later his grandchildren; they were exercised too for the benefit of the 'Men's Fellowship', on chapel outings and in fund-raising shows that the chapel-goers mounted to entertain one another. Though he moved outside the chapel community, and indeed he was constantly hailing acquaintances as he walked through Barnsley's streets or around Shaw Lane Cricket Ground on summer evenings, still it was the chapel community that his social life was centred on; and the chapel provided him with an arena that his vivacity could expand in contentedly.

By the same token his and my mother's devotion to reading did not make them odd fish in the congregation of Sheffield Road, neither in others' eyes nor in their own. Received opinion about provincial nonconformity would suggest otherwise, but as I cast my mind back to my boyhood I recall nothing sullen nor philistine about the Barnsley Baptists. The chapel was not just a religious and social focus, but a cultural focus too, and one that had easy and unsuspicious relations with the culture of the nation at large. My mother no more than my father felt isolated or out of place. In recent years when I have happily re-established contact with my native town, and have met again some who were chapel children along with me, I think I have perceived, though Sheffield Road chapel was long ago torn down, the same unflurried connections still being made between literary culture and the Dissenting religious allegiance. And this has provoked me into trying to find out why and when and how the contrary impression was created in the public mind, the impression that philistinism and religious nonconformity go together. When I lectured about this in Cambridge in 1976, I thought that I was keeping the faith with my mother and father.

My mother was 'literary' because it was through English literature, particularly English poetry, that she had risen to become a certificated school-teacher, without benefit of college training. But that gives the wrong impression. With her, as she might have said herself, English poetry was a passion. She had by heart the greater part, perhaps all, of *The Golden Treasury*, as well as much of Shelley, Browning, Tennyson, others. Tags of verses from Keats and Wordsworth, Shelley and Browning, were always in her mouth; and she was abreast of twentieth-century poets like Flecker and de la Mare, Masefield and Bridges, Drinkwater and W. H. Davies, Newbolt and Noyes. If I am so literary myself that I sometimes despair of breaking through a cocoon of words to a reality outside them, that is above all my mother's doing. And I am grateful, mostly; if my universe is verbal, so be it – I am happy in my glittering envelope, and will fight those who would puncture it.

My father, at the times that I remember best, was working long hours to keep his head and ours above water. I am speaking of the Depression. So he had no time for reading, and I thought him less literary than my mother. But if my copy of Burns is a first prize awarded to Alice Sugden of the Sheffield Road Baptist Sunday School, my *Poetical Works of Cowper* was in the same year, 1914, a first prize awarded to George C. Davie after a tennis tournament of the Park Tennis Club, Stainbrough. And I see now that their common bookishness was one thing that must have brought my parents together; I guess indeed that it was romantic literature, doubtless Sir Walter Scott, that impelled my father when he joined the colours in 1915 to enlist in the Highland Light Infantry. Fortunately for him, that regiment went to Gallipoli without him, and he was with the King's Own Scottish Borderers when he was wounded at Passchendaele. But he did his initial training in Edinburgh Castle, and ever afterwards Edinburgh was the metropolis of his imagination; though there was not a drop of Scottish blood in our veins, it was not London but Edinburgh that we all dreamed of visiting and indeed managed to visit just once. In later years when he had more leisure, my father once again read a great deal, often substantial works of biography and history. And always he too quoted favourite and for him sacred passages, particularly (as I recall) Wolsey's speech from Shakespeare's *Henry VIII*: 'Had I but served my God as I have served my King . . .'

John Masefield wrote of himself as one 'who belonged to a literary time, when all read much, and often found the delightful spoil of so much reading a hindrance when they came to tell a tale'. My mother and my father were representatives of that 'literary time', determined and zealous recruits to the idea of a literary civilization, each of them sprung from a family and a level of English society to which that idea had not penetrated earlier. They survived to know the very different world which had been heralded, before either of them was born, when a French poet had exhorted his fellows to 'take eloquence and wring its neck'. Though in fact my mind is laced through with tags and allusions less than theirs were, nevertheless, because I was willingly conditioned by their example, I seem, to others no doubt and certainly to myself, to be an anachronistic survival from that literary time, living and writing after them in a world in which the idea of a literary civilization is discredited and mocked almost universally, and through times in which the gap between that ideal and any achievable social reality is wider than they could have imagined. And I am stubborn about this, quite impenitent. That is one reason, I suppose, why I will not trust dreams to do for me what only a deliberately composed fable can do, convey wisdom by consistent allegory.

Louis Simpson tells how, growing up in Jamaica, he never knew that he was Jewish, or partly Jewish; and records how, if he had been told, he would not have known what to make of it, or how it was significant. So too in my boyhood 'the Jew' did not exist. Was there a synagogue in Barnsley? It seems to me that there wasn't, or else I should have heard of it. I'm not aware that I ever knew a single Jew until I was twenty years old. More pointedly, it now comes to me that on the contrary I probably did know such a one: Henry Hall, scoutmaster and Rugby football coach, who in those capacities (certainly not in the classroom, for his subject was chemistry, which bored me) did more for me than any of my other teachers in Barnsley Grammar School. Henry I. Hall . . . and the enigmatic initial, I now realize, doubtless stood for Isaac or Ira, for he had a Jewish physiognomy, and hailed from Leeds where Jews are numerous. The

14

telling circumstance is that at no time was the inference made, by me or any of my school-mates, nor so far as I know by any of our parents. So far was anti-semitism from being any part of our experience. If there was any sort of metaphysical ghetto in Barnsley, and a magical or uncanny people that dwelt within it, that role was played by the Roman Catholics, whom I was dimly and infrequently aware of as a minority, 'priest-ridden', who lived a life in some respects secret, different from the rest of us. Was this not a curious and almost touching survival, among twentieth-century Protestants in England, of a pattern of feeling that one associates rather with the seventeenth century, or the eighteenth? It meant at any rate that we grew up, I and my school-mates, in entire innocence of the age-old sore that just then, in the 1930s, was swelling and festering afresh, to be monstrously lanced in Germany by Hitler's 'final solution'. And my natural incredulity – that there was such a thing as a 'Jewish problem', let alone a problem that called for unthinkable solutions – survived into and all through the Second World War. When in 1945 the British and American armies, advancing into Germany, discovered appalling and irrefutable evidence of what we now call 'the holocaust', no one was more astonished than I was, except presumably some who had been brought up like me. I remember vividly – was it in Union Street in Devonport? – an exhibition of the photographs of liberated Belsen, its ovens and lime-pits, inspected quite on the off-chance by me, a sailor on shore-leave. When I have told people that my scepticism survived so long, they have found it hard to believe, so that now I have difficulty crediting my own memories. What needs to be understood is that, as an earnest and high-minded schoolboy, I had been urged to read, and had read, books like Norman Angell's *The Great Illusion* which supported their anti-militarism by telling of war propaganda and atrocity stories, of Horatio Bottomley in the First World War, and reports of German Uhlans with Belgian babies on their lances. Inevitably, therefore, as the stories of anti-Jewish atrocities filtered through in the 1940s, I thought I knew better than to believe them! I need not draw any of the too obvious morals: how right-minded propaganda can rather disastrously misfire; or – more disconcertingly still – how enlightened and liberal attitudes will be lamed, almost inevitably, by an inability to conceive of Evil as a real principle, the positive force and drive of simple depravity.

But I'm not interested in drawing morals, have not the heart for it. Instead I am overcome with simple sorrow for the innocence we all had, my parents too – an innocence that is still to be found in one or two English people I know, for which alas there is nowadays no excuse. We thought we were enlightened and knowledgeable, even sceptical; and by comparison with many of our neighbours, so we were. But all that reasonableness played over a foundation of unexamined certainties – not least,the certainty that one could be proud of being British, since the British Empire had been and still was the most enlightened and enlightening of all empires the world had seen. This showed how provincial we were; for a poet whose work had not yet penetrated to us, W. H. Auden, was already expressing, with a dry distaste that deepened into horror, the quite different climate that was to reign in England after the war – not knowledgeability but knowingness, not open-minded scepticism but the preconceived conviction that things are never what they seem, there is always a dirty secret and a story not yet told, and whatever seems noble and honourable is always a lie. Disillusioned perhaps, disenchanted certainly, I mourn the loss of real or seeming certainties.

It was Robin Hood country, all of it – in a way that I always knew, yet had not recalled nor seen any point in recalling, until I lately read Frank Morley's *Literary Britain*, where he makes fascinatingly much of the tension, in the historical imagination of the English, between King Arthur on the one hand, Robin Hood on the other. My mother was of those to whom Tennyson's *Idylls of the King* meant much, and I hear her now in sunny mood evoking

> Elaine the fair, Elaine the lovable,
> Elaine the lily-maid of Astolat . . .

not to speak of 'The Lady of Shalott'; yet it was surely she who bought me on my seventh birthday the large and boldly illustrated *Stories of Robin Hood* which, read and re-read through ensuing years, surely did more than any other single text to make me a compulsive reader for ever after. (The book, I am delighted to discover, is still in print; so that a few years ago I was able to make a present of it to my first grandson.) And indeed, now that I think about it, there was a smaller *Stories of King Arthur*, bought for me amid great excitement on my part in a long-vanished bookshop in Church Street in Barnsley, which mysteriously failed to deliver pleasures to equal or even approach those of Robin Hood. I must be careful not to rig the evidence in retrospect, so as to fall in with Frank Morley's so seductive thesis. And yet, though I bear never so hard and sceptically on my boyhood memories, they do indeed support his suggestion – that north and east of a line that he identifies daringly with the highway A6, the ancient Watling Street, Robin Hood plays in the folk-memory the role that south and west of that line is played by the in many ways incompatible figure of King Arthur. I have certainly misrepresented my parents if I have given the impression that in them folk-memories persisted with any unreflecting sturdiness. For experience of that I had to wait for my

16

mother-in-law, who would say, 'This place looks like Troytown', without any knowledge of, or curiosity about, the bequest through generations that brought that phrase to her lips. And she, so far as we could determine – for she had as little interest in familial as in any other antiquity – hailed from the heart of King Arthur country, 'woning far by the west'. No, it is precisely because my parents made it a point of honour not to harbour in their imaginations things their reason could not endorse, that the insistent presence of Robin Hood in their and therefore in my consciousness seems significant. For, beyond the commonplace of 'robbing the rich to give to the poor', nothing was forthcoming from them to explain why Robin Hood cropped up so continually in our shared experience – why, for instance, 'Robin Hood's Stride' was the name of a curious rocky outcrop above and behind the Derbyshire farm between Bakewell and Winster that my mother's schoolmistress friends made available to us for family holidays. And there was, I remember, an item surely brought home by my father from a second-hand bookshop in Shambles Street; an edition of Robin Hood ballads which was, I suppose, as indigestible for my parents as it always was for me – because it was 'scholarly', and accordingly reproduced Middle English orthography which none of us could pronounce.

Frank Morley is the first author I have come across who explains something that I remember mildly puzzling about when I was in my teens: the geographical *stretch* of the Robin Hood associations. If Sherwood Forest was Robin's haunt, as every one averred and as my *Stories of Robin Hood* was quite insistent about, then how explain Robin Hood's Bay, many miles away on the Yorkshire coast? Or for that matter – what I knew, and was moved by – his famous and tragic death right in our neighbourhood, at Kirklees Priory, near Wakefield? Morley casts the topographical net still wider, and defines as Robin's territory – on good evidence, apparently – the Inglewood or 'Englysche wood', way to the north-west, past Penrith or Carlisle. Morley's explanation, which I haven't the learning to contest, seems to be that the area of Robin's predominance corresponds to that of the ancient Danelaw; and his arguments – not presented as arguments but only as intriguing suggestions, which is all that the topic permits of – are sufficiently compelling. Yet, so far does he persuade me to cast aside the teenage cockiness which judged for instance Robin Hood's Bay to be nothing more than the bright idea of a Victorian realtor, that I dare to wonder if the rivalry between King Arthur and Robin Hood does not go deeper, and reach further back: to the rivalry between an agricultural (hence, neolithic) and a woodland culture. Robin of Locksley's 'greenwood' preserves the memory of an era before the forest was cleared, hacked down and fenced, for the neolithic farmer to assert his cropping and his grazing rights. If this seems a far call from the world of Arthur Scargill and the National Union of Mineworkers, one must recall that it is those same 'greenwoods', forests long buried and compressed, which now deliver coal.

At this rate I seem to have learned, too late to be much use, the mythic dimension of location and residence. Though now I live in the West Country, in the realm of King Arthur, it begins to seem that that will always be the wrong England for me.

2

Northerners

From Barnsley there runs north and south an unbroken chain of squalid little townships, the meanly built and hastily improvised barracks of the Industrial Revolution, all the way from Sheffield up to Leeds and beyond. But west and east it is a different, more hopeful story. Westward in particular – and we lived on the west side of town – the land begins to rise at once, through Dodworth and Silkstone and Hoylandswaine; and then, after a dip into Penistone, which is already a windy upland town, it rises steeply again to become after a few miles uncultivated and largely trackless Pennine moorland. Though coal is mined on the lower slopes, so that Silkstone indeed gives its name to the whole seam, yet the look and feel of the country, once you are through Dodworth, is quite different. Hoylandswaine for instance is lean and rinsed and raking. There are seventeenth-century farmhouses thereabouts, all the better for being merely bare and solid, the harshness of weather giving no purchase for creepers or lichens any more than the harshness of livelihood could afford Jacobean curlicues. The stone is good, a washed-out yellow in some lights very faintly pink. And in particular, near to Hoylandswaine but off the main road and until lately away from any metalled road at all, there is the vast tithe-barn of Gunthwaite, little known and little visited, still indeed a barn. Going from Barnsley to Hoylandswaine, though it is less than ten miles and one is travelling west rather than north, one moves out of the Midlands decisively into the North, the North Country as I came to know it later in Wharfedale, Nidderdale, Swaledale, and in the poems of Wordsworth and Emily Brontë. To me and to my brother – for I know that on this issue I can speak for him – it has been important that we should define ourselves as Northerners, of that 'North'.

And 'north' is a metaphysical or else a metaphorical place – in this sense: that wherever in the Northern hemisphere one writes from, northward is the region of the stripped and the straitened, the necessitous. It was many years later that I realized this, seeing what 'north' and 'northward' meant in the poems of William Stafford, who speaks his poems always from some place on an axis between Kansas and Oregon. And it was years later again that I reflected how odd it must be to be an Australian, for whom the north is, I suppose, a region of tropical luxury. This metaphor of 'the northern' has meant much to me, since as far back as I can remember; what may look in my later life like a considered opting

19

for the spare and the lean – in intellectual style or in literary style – is in truth, I think, only a clinging close on my part to that northern metaphor which I have agreed with myself to trust through thick and thin.

From that North – still literal, though already metaphorical also – I came in 1940 to Cambridge, on scholarships and exhibitions that I had won through fierce competition. It had been for too many years the pinpointed objective of my own and my parents' ambitions; it was impossible that Cambridge, or any other place, should have lived up to the hope that we had placed upon it. And to this day I cannot tell how much of the rancorous unhappiness which I often feel when I am in Cambridge harks back to the predictable and inevitable disappointment that it was to me forty years ago. I expected too much of that town and its university; and if I still expect flagrantly more than it has to give, that is, I dare say, devious and twisted testimony to the love and the loyalty that I invested in it. But it is with a bad grace, and reluctantly, that I concede so much. For its complacency seems as impregnable now as it was all those years ago. Some time in that span of years I arrived at the diagnosis which I adhere to still: that the Cantabrigian ethos – is it Cromwellian? I persuade myself with some gratification that it is – leaves no margin for *caprice*, for that free-running, freely associating, arbitrary and gratuitous play of mind out of which, not exclusively but necessarily, art-works arise. This is a diagnosis which undercuts such comfortably intra-mural altercations as Kathleen Raine's with William Empson, or F. R. Leavis's with C. P. Snow.

To a Northerner such as I believed myself to be, or was determined on being – one moreover who, as it happened, had been reared a Baptist – a

'In our North Country'

Cromwellian ethos should have had, and in some measure it did have, obvious attractions. It would certainly appear that Cambridge was more appropriately my university, than Oxford would have been (though, needless to say, in the scholarship competition I was happy to settle for either place, and what Oxford might have done for me, or done *to* me, who can say?). Undoubtedly when, in my second term, I was supervised by Joan Bennett in her house at Church Rate Corner in Newnham, the somewhat self-applauding stringency of the Cambridge ethos, and its disputatiousness, were very much to my taste; I felt secure and at home with these fashions of intellectual life.

But already I go too fast, or I fly too high. 'Cromwellian', that 'ethos' . . . what do they have to do, such words, with the timid and entranced schoolboy who first saw Cambridge at Easter 1940? Already timid, already entranced, I had changed trains at Peterborough or March, and had spun on, alone in the compartment, eyes wide and intent over the erstwhile undreamed-of fenlands. I was to sit the Scholarship examinations, and would sleep for three nights over one of the spick and span shops in King's Parade. Two or three others were there with me, and one was Arnold Edinborough. It must have been with Arnold and another that I sallied forth that first evening to wander, in the dank but luminous twilight, among college buildings of which I remember for certain only the Bridge of Sighs in St Johns. That evening, if never since, Cambridge lived up to my expectations. And yet that is wrong too. For I had no preconceptions: the place was all a wonder, and I all wonderment before it – as I could not have been had I moved in my schooldays through medieval or Victorian cloisters. That some schools boasted such things, I knew from school stories by Gunby Hadath and Hylton Cleaver; and at that time I looked to Cambridge to redeem for me promissory notes in no currency any sounder than that! This meant that the youth who wrote for the examiners could be precociously fluent just because he wrote for them about things that were quite unreal to him once he was out in the street. This living of two lives, or of one life on two such different levels, did not worry me. I was an athlete of the examination hall, and duplicities like making-a-little-go-a-long-way were what I had exultantly trained myself in. I took as much pleasure in this sport as my schoolfellows did on the running track or the football field, where for that matter I could perform creditably enough but never so as to excel. My mother, whose pleasure in this was as uncomplicated as my own, would tell with relish of the tradesman's errand-boy at her kitchen door who, being asked if he knew me in school, replied: 'Him! He poozzles t'gaffers.' I have had friends later in my life who, having come up the same way, had the same robust and grateful attitude to the examination system. This way we had come up by did not seem to us a *hard* way, and even today when I hear this way and this system deplored as 'élitist', as 'competitive', as 'meritocracy', I wonder sardonically why these brickbats are never thrown on to the tennis court or into the swimming pool. I can still at times recover, when I write a review or deliver an important lecture, the old triumphant pleasure at putting-all-the-goods-in-the-shop-window, living dangerously, outwitting the examiner/reader. None of my children share this competitive appetite, and insofar as they are aware of it in me perhaps at times they dislike it; I do not often upbraid them for that, I only regret for their sake that they miss the pleasure of it.

On the other hand, outside of my studies, Cambridge in 1940 seemed to be peopled or at any rate dominated by exquisites from King's or swells from Trinity; and these were people so far beyond the horizons of my previous experience that I regarded them from afar with uncomprehending resentment and alarm. It was with nothing short of terror that one summer evening I saw a tall pair of them, drunk, negotiating the turn from Bene't Street into King's Parade. I felt very vulnerable indeed – far from home, and quite at sea among modes and codes of behaviour of which I had no experience, and to which I had no key. That an unusually stupid member of my college should once or twice in hall have tried to snub me, an exhibitioner, as himself a fee-paying commoner, is doubtless an interesting item of social history. But it wasn't fatuities of that sort which dismayed and bewildered me. The cleavage was not along the lines of income, nor of *class*; I was lower middle class, and knew it, and before long came to see that most of my Home Counties fellow undergraduates were petty bourgeois also. The cleavage, the divide, was not social but cultural, in the anthropologist's sense of 'culture'; to give a ludicrous instance, I and my first friend, Arnold Edinborough from Lincolnshire, suffered through many weeks of our first term before we realized that our provincial ritual of High Tea about five in the afternoon could not be reconciled, without digestive discomfort, with the institution of dinner in Hall two hours later. In crucial matters like these – and they are crucial, since they are matters of daily rhythm, how it is punctuated and thereby ritualized – the Cromwellian university was as alien to us Northern provincials as ever Royalist High Church Oxford could have been.

Arnold was buoyantly ready to 'take on' more of Cambridge than I was. I dare say he was as ready to latch on to me as I was on to him, when as freshmen we recognized each other. But at the time it felt like a very unequal friendship, with Arnold munificently giving what I gratefully received. Certainly it was he who, ebullient and apparently assured and already almost portly, carried the pair of us into fields of college and university life that I lacked the confidence to broach on my own – into for instance the college Boat Club, which I precipitately retired from after two weeks' experience of the semi-military discipline it exacted. (That I had enough of in any case, in the compulsory parades with the Training Corps, unrelievedly wretched hours.) I may once even have been dragged by Arnold to an audition for one of the Dramatic Societies. At all events Arnold was all zest and curiosity, passing on to me in an affectionately jeering way all the information that he avidly sought out concerning nuances and alignments in the social life of the undergraduates. Though it was I and not he who had won an award from the Scholarship examination, yet it was on him, I thought, that fortune smiled, and always would. Typical for instance was the sorry contrast between the college lodgings that had been assigned to me and the spacious airy rooms that had come his way, in Pemberton Terrace off Brookside. Though I remember to be sure that the pair of us toasted crumpets over my gas-fire, and ate them with *patum pepperium*, yet it seems to me that I spent all my leisure hours in Pemberton Terrace where Mrs Alderton, unlike my landlady, had certain refined mannerisms that reminded me reassuringly of my mother. In Pemberton Terrace, I saw, Arnold would be able to entertain as many bloods and aesthetes as he pleased, as soon as he had mastered (as he would and I wouldn't) the mysterious conventions of their behaviour. Arnold comes back to me now, in early afternoon sunlight flooding that room, singing:

> By brooks too broad for leaping
> The lightfoot lads are laid;
> The rose-lipped girls are sleeping
> In fields where roses fade.

Sixteen years later I visited him and his wife Letty in Kingston, Ontario; but I've lost contact with him since, though I believe he became for a while something of a household word in television-watching Canada.

It was of course with him, and the three other St Catharine's freshmen reading English, that at 9 o'clock one sunny brisk October morning I waited on my first supervisor, the medievalist H. S. Bennett, in Emmanuel. All wearing our newly purchased college scarves, we foregathered in the modest elegance of Emmanuel's neo-classical court; and then and there I met someone who was to bulk in my later life more largely than Arnold Edinborough, more largely indeed than any one outside my family. This was Douglas Brown, who in the memories of those who knew him stands out more sharply than the record of his career, or his one and only book (on Thomas Hardy), seems to give warrant for. Douglas was smallish and low-voiced, with a darting grace in all his quick movements. Over his bony forehead waved a lock of lank but not quite straight

23

black hair. The lower part of his face was strongly marked, with a jowl not heavy but prominent and even then, when he was so young, blue-black after the closest shave. This, if only we had known at that first meeting, was the telling feature: the muscular prominence about the mouth. For it was when he spoke rapidly in his quiet voice, that everyone was astonished. I have never, before or since, encountered such a gift for articulation, and in the strictest sense; for his vocabulary was wide, fastidious and choice, but what was remarkable was the marshalling of that vocabulary in spoken syntax, the leaping and springing clauses that unwound luxuriantly, crossed over, and yet drew unerringly home. It was daunting, and finding it in a fellow-student I was daunted indeed. He spoke like a book, as someone said in my Yorkshire boyhood, meaning however a sort of speech leaden-footed and pedantic, as Douglas's was not. When he wrote his book, the book spoke like a man, like the man who was the author – all too much so. For I speak of the luxuriant first draft; what was published was the result of a surgical pruning so savage that, along with the idiosyncrasy, much of the life went out of it. F. R. Leavis's pages speak out at us like that, as Douglas's first pages did. And that is no accident. For Leavis in his day, and Douglas in his, had been tutored at the Perse school, there in Cambridge, by a schoolmaster seemingly of genius, Caldwell Cook, who required that the boys' compositions be *voiced*, not read aloud but delivered before the class as close-knit and memorized orations. Douglas's extraordinary facility must I think have been innate, but Caldwell Cook had strengthened and refined it.

As I became more intimate with Douglas, my relations with Arnold came under strain. If Arnold was ever bowled over by Douglas, and prepared to bow to a precocious erudition such as we'd none of us encountered before in a contemporary, the submission did not last for long. He soon had his suspicions, which from his point of view were well-founded. For it was from Douglas, not Arnold, that I began to get the clear message that my two friendships were incompatible. Nothing was said, however. From a talker so prompt and fluent as Douglas, and so copious, having nothing to say was itself an unmistakable and ominous signal. And when Arnold was of the company, or when his name came up in conversation, Douglas's sudden taciturnity, the chill that came from him, the abrupt withdrawal of attention and interest, sounded like a thunderclap. What's more, I realized with wonderment that a signal was indeed being sent, that Douglas's aversion to my other friend may or may not have been spontaneous, but his conveying of it was certainly deliberate. Also it was directed – at me. So I recognized that what was at issue was nothing so trivial as jealousy; Douglas had decided that Arnold was 'bad for me', and was registering his disapproval so as to set me on a better track. Not without resentment I perceived that I was being 'moulded', by this cool customer of my own age! So I apprehended for the first time what all who knew Douglas came in time to recognize – that behind the quiet demureness, the always accommodating good manners, the self-effacing dowdiness of Douglas's dress and even his demeanour, the personality was authoritarian, even predatory. In time, with those who knew him well, he did not bother to conceal this. Years later, when he had taken a double starred First in the Tripos and then quixotically elected for schoolmastering in his old school, he explained his decision by citing the Jesuits' maxim to the effect that, having charge of a young person between eight and fourteen (or whatever the ages are), you could mark him for life. And at the same time he said to Doreen and me: 'Don't think I have any illusions about little boys. First bash their heads together to show them who's in charge, and then you can teach them something.' Later again I taught as undergraduates some of Douglas's pupils from the Perse, and saw how deep an imprint he had left on them, how they mimed without knowing it his manners and mannerisms. When our own son went through that school, we were secretly relieved that it so happened Douglas never taught him. (But Mark remembers him all the same, quite vividly – remembers how, thanks to his wearing sandals and dark-coloured shirts, Douglas had the ability, very disconcerting in a school-

My parents with their grandson: Dodworth Road, Barnsley, *c.* 1953

master, of suddenly materializing at a schoolboy's elbow, addressing him with soft precision.)

It is hardly too much to say that then, in 1940, Douglas was already recruiting for a cause, and had picked on me as likely material. We now know that at the same time, or only a few years before, Anthony Blunt and perhaps some others, in a different sector of the same university, were recruiting for a different ideology, and picking on some who were likely material for treason. Some years ago, before Blunt had been un-masked, mischievous rumour, printed in a Sunday newspaper, wrongly identified the recruiter for the K.G.B. as Donald Beves, one of two Fellows of King's who were prominent in the councils and the productions of the Marlowe Society. This false identification shows what circles of the Uni-versity are thought to have been those where traitors were recruited. I remember Beves as a splendid Pandarus in *Troilus and Cressida*, and years later as a less than splendid Macduff, his knees bony under an implaus-ible kilt. And it was when Arnold, while not surrendering his multifarious interests in the University, applied himself particularly to acting with the Marlowe Society, that Douglas's disapproval of him sharpened. Arnold, the burly yeoman and largely unreflecting Tory, was no sort of likely material for treacherous espionage. And Douglas had no way of know-ing, more than anyone else, what the Anthony Blunts were up to. All the same he smelled, coming from the circles that Arnold aspired to and modestly broke into, something that might have been called 'decadent' or 'licentious', if not quite 'depraved'. Douglas did not use these words; and yet the conditions that they point at seemed to him – so I now reconstruct the matter – waiting at the end of the road that Arnold, intoxicated with the histrionic glamour of Cambridge, had set his feet upon. That glamour was of course spurious, as all such glamours must be – though less vulgarly so, I cannot help feeling, in those days when one said or sang Housman's lyrics than nowadays when T.V. viewers have seen on their screens a Cambridge converted to soap-opera under the title, *The Glittering Prizes*. But for Douglas spuriousness was seamless and indivisible: once tolerate the tinsel in little things, and one would come to accept the factitious all across the board. Just that indeed was the first and determining dogma of the ideology he was recruiting for. And although this was held as dogma, he would have said (and I came to agree) that it was demonstrable – and in just that field of experience, literature, which had brought us together. For a poem, even the longest of poems, was physically a little thing; yet thanks to the powers and graces of language it was either a microcosm or else at least an intense focus, a burning-glass, wherein were collected the beams of a reality much wider than itself. A splotch or stain of tinsel in the glass would skew and falsify all that wider field which it drew into itself. And as with the behaviour of language in a poem, so with the behaviour of a man or a woman in any situation, even the most trivial. How can that logic be broken, except at the cost of pushing literature and poetry into a merely marginal or optional status in the field of human endeavour? That question, which began to confound me then, has not ceased to baffle me since. Though my style in print and in the lecture-hall has long been assured and trenchant, still I seem to myself to waver somewhere in the middle between Arnold and Douglas. Where was the place for instance, in Douglas's scheme of things, for those verses that Arnold's light baritone carolled so happily? 'By brooks too broad for leaping . . .' – it is tinsel language, surely. Must it then be set down as not unimportant merely, but *vicious*? Douglas would go as far as that, and it followed from his way of thinking, which was F. R. Leavis's, that poems by Housman which were by any account more important because more powerful were by just that token more dangerous, and so more vicious. Though Douglas Brown and F. R. Leavis are dead, this way of thinking about literature, though it offends the majority as it always did, is still alive and thriving; and I cannot regret that. It informs for instance many of the mostly admirable teaching manuals in literature that are distributed from the Open University. And as of old so now, it persuades me least when it offers to 'place' the minor achievements of a Housman say, a Robert Bridges or a Robert Graves. Though it is no argument, still it is somehow to the point that I know from experience how hard it is to turn a lyric stanza as gracefully as these writers do. In any case there must be something wrong with a way of thinking that has such difficulty finding room for the thoroughly creditable though less than momentous performance. And yet on the other hand, as we learn more about what was going on in some privileged sectors of the Cambridge of that time, words like 'vicious' or 'decadent', even 'depraved', seem less obviously intemperate than they did even a few years ago.

But it is a far cry back, in time and in experience, from the specious security of such diagnoses, to what it felt like to be, in Cambridge in 1940, walking for the first or the twentieth time across Coe Fen. As always, memory shies at the daunting challenge – what was it like *then*? what was it like *there*? – and runs for cover into recalling instead images of some use to social history or the history of ideas: the bookshop in Rose Crescent which proffered Stalinist paperbacks to remind us that the University had housed, not many months before, Julian Bell and John Cornford; or the gaping house in Grantchester Meadows where a returning German bomber one night loosed off a stray bomb.

Our concerns – I speak for my close friends, Arnold and Douglas and Stanley Lockett – were hardly at all political, as they surely would have been only eighteen months before, but covertly sexual. Only Stanley I believe dared to confront his sexual needs with anything but tormented chastity. Mine were focussed, by no means satisfactorily, on the person of a Colchester Baptist's daughter, from Homerton, with whom I walked out demurely on Sunday afternoons towards Grantchester and Coton. Douglas too at that time had a steady girl-friend; and it would be three or four years yet before he confessed to himself and to her that his bent was homosexual, a proclivity which he rigorously refused to satisfy.

Douglas's home, his parents' home, was in Sedley Taylor Road. And more than one summer evening of 1941 saw the two Northerners, Stanley and me, lagging none too willingly along the privet-hedges of Hills Road and Sedley Taylor Road, heading for the feast of exotic culture – mostly, music on records – that Douglas, eager and impulsive, would have cooked up for us. Already at that time I knew I was going to join up, and that I only had to rationalize my way out of the principled pacifism of Douglas, and of the sectarian club, the Robert Hall Society, that I had joined without enthusiasm. In the event Douglas was in uniform before I was, as a medical orderly in the R.A.F.; and it was later that same summer that I spent some hours with him in Harrogate, where he had been posted and (as he told me without complaint) read *The Brothers Karamazov* in the intervals of swabbing floors. One weekend leave he stayed with me in Barnsley; and I have a vision of my mother beaming happily as he tried (without success) to persuade me that Ronald Bottrall's *Festivals of Fire* deserved all that Leavis had claimed for it.

Sometimes it seems to me that if there is one sort of rhetoric for which I have been fitted by nature as well as nurture, it is the Jeremiad. I have made a comfortable career out of crying in saturnine tones, 'Woe! woe!' or 'It is later than you think', or 'Things are going from bad to worse'. And a whole generation of English writers grew up along with me in this modestly profitable skill. The best of us are those, like Kingsley Amis or Bernard Levin or Anthony Burgess, who mock their own gloomy irascibility even as they articulate it. And this is only just; by whipping their own exasperations to comic or farcical fury, such writers very happily belie their own premises. For the elation of comedy is saying hooray for life in its own terms, however incongruous and absurd. But this was not anything I learned from Cambridge, or in Cambridge – where on the contrary everyone seemed to be caught still in Matthew Arnold's dilemma: how to find room, in a theory of literature which turned upon 'high seriousness', for the great masters of the comic vision, for Chaucer and Burns, Dickens and Aristophanes. There was to be sure Leonard Potts of Queens' College, author of a modest handbook, *Comedy*, which still supplies the best account known to me of why Congreve's dialogue in *The Way of the World* is not just a classic of the English theatre, but poetic also. But in 1940 and for years thereafter one was unmistakably aware that Mr Potts, so easily as he could be disconcerted, so manifestly idiosyncratic as he was in his habits and his bearing, was not to be taken seriously. Comedy in fact, though it is surely one of the two or three canonical modes in which the human imagination has made sense of the human condition, has never yet been accommodated by the Cambridge mind, happily as that mind can lend itself to the really quite disparate mode of dry and pungent wit. And so, unlike the Amises and the Burgesses and the Levins, we Cantabrigian Jeremiahs, who have the gift of comedy only fitfully or not at all – we are all too often pompous and boring, and self-pitying too.

It is thus that I reflect with dismay, reading over these lacklustre pages that I have devoted to Cambridge, and to the first year that I spent there. How stale I have made it seem! Were there no exaltations, no transports? There were; and it is only the insidiously habitual rhetoric that makes me pass over them. Let me single out one at least. I think of the English Faculty Library at Cambridge, in the rear of the Old Schools. I remember as magical the first visits that I paid to it. So many books! Other freshmen may have been daunted by them, but I exulted in their number. They were all mine if I chose to make them so, every one of them guaranteed to bear in upon and enrich the proclivity that I knew to be, and had declared to be, my own. Therefore there was no question of choosing. Any shelf, chosen at random, would do as well as any other. And, as I recall vividly, the shelf I chose was given over to seventeenth-century pulpit oratory. Why not? One tome after another, the histories and critical commentaries were lugged out to my bicycle-basket, and conveyed to my cramped and cluttered 'digs' in Marlowe Road. (And what wickedly exact fun, I now remember, Arnold Edinborough made of how my West Riding accent handled the vowels of 'Marlowe Road'!) I was never disappointed. No book of scholarship could disappoint me then. The more recondite the information, the more it entranced me. And so it is still, or would be if I could clear enough time around me; the romance of scholarship is in its exoticism, not in its rigour. The only trouble was when to stop; and it was a real trouble, the worst trouble of student life – today I feel for those of my students who are going to be scholars, as time after time I have to wrench their heads around, jarringly, from one subject or theme or field of interest to what the curriculum declares to be the next in order.

Education! I have no thoughts about education; or else I have too many thoughts, all of them Jeremiah's. Sometimes, certainly, it happens in classrooms: at Barnsley Grammar School, in the classroom of 'Fiery'

Evans, intense diminutive Welshman whose irascibility, though it was all a pedagogue's tactical histrionics, drove the structure of the French language into my consciousness at a level where nothing will root it out; and in the classroom of Frank Merrin, whose tactic on the contrary was suavity, as he supplied a skeletal history of French literature. But mostly education, the sort that I care about, happens in libraries. And I am grateful to every library I have known: to Barnsley Public Library, especially its reference room, where I read with delight how the battle of Brunanburh, subject of an Old English poem that I have never read and never shall read, may have been fought somewhere between Barnsley and Rotherham; to a weirdly dusty and unpeopled library in Archangel, North Russia, where afternoon sunlight in the summer of 1943 slanted on Tauchnitz editions of F. Marion Crawford; to the library of St Catharine's College, which yielded me a splendid edition of Fanny Burney's *Evelina*; to the library of Caius, where I annotated through much of a long vacation the Sidney Psalter along with John Ruskin's exultant comments upon it; to the neglected but still handsome and surprising library of the Union Society in Cambridge; even the Cambridge University Library, unfriendlist of all; the public library of Plymouth, destroyed in the blitz on Devonport, healing itself slowly through long years after the war; and certainly the library of Trinity College Dublin, housed incomparably in and below the barrel-vaulted Long Room that is one of the noblest rooms in the world, its symbolically long perspective enforced by matching lines of white marble busts, some of them by Scheemakers, some by Roubiliac.

From the moment I got to Cambridge, nothing did I hear from my teachers but 'tradition'. It was represented as something problematical, hard to get hold of, easily confounded with impostures. In particular it was supposed that I began with a prejudice against it, against the cloudiest concept of what it might be. But had Marlowe not lived in Corpus, James Shirley in St Catharine's, Wordsworth in St John's? Did I, then and there among the colleges, having won my way there out of the benighted provinces, need T. S. Eliot or F. R. Leavis or later Richard Hoggart to tell me on what terms to accept incorporation in the tradition there offered me, physically extant in the disposition of buildings and in book-stacks? Preaching at me, these authorities preached to the converted; and the long-converted grew to resent them. Now, in retrospect, I recognize how I must thank my parents for having saved me from the sterile class-rancour that got in the way of so many of my contemporaries, and impedes their successors to the present day. Since disputatiousness was in Cambridge a sign of 'integrity', and since it came happily and naturally to my cast of mind, I indulged it – to good and profitable effect. But it never truly mirrored my temperament or my sensibility, by which I knew that the tradition was *there*, in Cambridge; and that the custodians of it were not pedagogues and critics, but poets, libraries, and the builders of libraries.

The builders. . . . It was years later, after the war was over, that a student of the Bartlett School of Architecture took a group of us round the colleges, and expatiated on the audacity of Wren's library in Trinity. I have always been grateful to him; but grateful also to Norris Jubb, who returned from South America to be art-master in Barnsley Grammar School, whom in his last decline I visited in his semi-detached two doors away from my parents' house. For it was Norris Jubb, organizing excursions to Romanesque and Gothic churches in the West Riding and down into Lincolnshire, who did more than anyone else to open up for me the other art that I respond to fervently outside of the literary arts – that is to say, architecture. What a gift that has proved to be! Bookish as I am and am proud to be, my response to the semblance that architecture creates, what Susanne Langer calls 'the ethnic domain', is what has enabled me time and again to declare myself a man *pour qui le monde visible existe*. Few of my literary contemporaries at Cambridge could declare as much; and, lacking that sort of purchase on the physically present and manifest, they have been the more vulnerable to the beguiling abstractions of the behavioural scientists and the cheap indignations of professional humanitarians, for whom 'tradition' is a formulaic manoeuvre of the enemy, a danger-signal. Cromwell's iconoclastic roundheads destroyed not architecture so much as the 'graven images' of sculpture; and after my first visit to Italy in 1952 it came home to me that, however Cromwellian I might be by virtue of my sectarian upbringing, this was one area in which I was not Cromwellian at all. In the 1950s Douglas Brown came to stay with us in Dublin, and I realized then that – conscientiously well-informed as Douglas was on sculpture, painting and architecture as on other matters – the moments when I interrupted our animated discussions to ask him to *see* such and such a coign or portico were endured by him as dutiful divagations from what were to him matters of real import, which is to say, literature and music. And so I came to recognize how an education in literature, so far from being an introduction to the world of artistic endeavour generally, could be on the contrary a way of evading the challenge presented to us by artifacts in stone or in pigment; and how a specifically Cambridge way of putting privileged emphasis on the *verbal* arts could lead to just that ultimately philistine conclusion. I see now that a course of lectures regularly given by my St Catharine's tutor T. R. Henn, on Painting in relation to Literature, was designed to obviate just that depressing condition; but in my own case it didn't work that way, and Henn's lectures did nothing at that time to elevate painting, for me, above the level of knowledgeable connoisseurship.

Not so with that earlier sidelong indoctrination by Norris Jubb! That infection really *took* – partly, I think, because going to look at churches could be happily combined, by a schoolboy, with the energetic independence of cycling thirty or forty miles on a Saturday afternoon on the bicycles, sturdy upright 'roadsters' with no gear but one, that I and my schoolfriends wheedled our parents into buying for us on our twelfth or thirteenth birthdays. Eastward was the way – to Hickleton, Barnburgh, Marr, villages just short of Doncaster. Barnburgh church in particular, which I haven't seen in more than forty years, was a dark and eerie cavern of massive Romanesque. Further afield, our furthest reach in a day's riding, was Selby Minster, the other side of Pontefract. And more than once I think, in another direction, we passed through Hampole, Richard Rolle's village, though I don't remember a church there.

Though usually my two companions on these trips were nonconformists as I was, it never occurred to us to think that medieval ecclesiastical England belonged to our Church of England contemporaries more than to us. We supposed ourselves no doubt, so far as we thought of it at all, blithe young free-thinkers. But sectarianism might have coloured our cultural sense, though it had no other substance. It didn't. And unlike the speaker of Philip Larkin's 'Churchgoing', I knew at fifteen 'what rood-lofts were'. A few years later, as a college freshman I could still make little of any buildings from the past 500 years, feeling sure in Cambridge that I was in the presence of architecture only with such authenticated pre-Renaissance monuments as the Round Church, or St Bene't's, with its Saxon tower. But the rudiments had been inculcated, the affection implanted. I have always been grateful.

And probably this is the best place to attend to a question that has sometimes been put to me: whether my defection from the Christian communion that I was reared in was not some sort of crucial watershed in my experience of life. The truth is, it was not: an answer that may reflect little credit on me, but hardly more on the nonconformist persuasion that I left. Such imperceptible and charitably tolerated leakings away of the Dissenting faithful seem to have been the rule among Dissenters of my generation, and of the one or two generations before me: Kingsley Martin, later the influential and mischievous editor of *The New Statesman*, and Philip Mairet, the less influential editor of the *New English Weekly*, were two older men who seem to have gone the same way. The still mysterious emancipation from the Plymouth Brethren of a more redoubtable figure, Allan Upward, is another case that may or may not – the evidence is still to seek – fall into the same pattern. Breaking with the inherited scheme should have mattered more than it did; should have been in fact a *break*, rather than what it was – a slide, an imperceptible glissade.

The truth seems to be that by 1900, or 1910, or 1920, the once so powerful Dissenting Interest in English society had so identified itself with the Liberal party in British politics that with the collapse and disintegration of the party the Dissenting Interest disintegrated also. My grandfather and, with significantly less ardour, my father were Lloyd George Liberals. In my boyhood the newspaper we took and mildly swore by was the Liberal *Daily News*, attending especially, if I remember aright, to its foreign correspondent and roving political commentator Vernon Bartlett.

And yet, if I'm to take at all seriously Frank Morley's mapping of a 'Robin Hood' territory in England, that Danelaw wedge aimed from the north and east at London and sharpened by for instance both John Bunyan and D. H. Lawrence, is there not, mythically, a drastic anomaly in that wedge being driven to promote David Lloyd George? That Welsh wizard, from Criccieth under the shoulder of Arthurian Snowdon – what was *he* doing, as the preferred bandit-leader of the greenwood bands of Robin Hood? To be sure, he too sprang from protestant Dissent – but of an eccentric sort, and with a distinctively Welsh accent that should have rung outlandishly in West Riding ears.

What even Frank Morley and more certainly others like E. P. Thompson fail to hear in the voice of English Dissent is the profoundly loyal and loyalist, monarchist, note. In the Robin Hood stories that I was given to read, as in many of the traditional ballads that they were based on, the antagonism to the hierarchical authorities of bishop and sheriff rests on, and is validated by, an allegiance to 'the true King' – which is to say, Richard the Lionheart, as against King John. And thus, when the Nonconformist–Liberal consensus split apart, on the disastrous political career of the ageing Lloyd George, there was as much reason to go with the loyalist Right as with the sentimentally republican Left. Yet the first possibility is mostly overlooked by students of English Dissent, who will have it that an allegiance to nonconformity in religion necessarily goes along with a Leftist orientation in politics. The alternative alignment is what I saw in my father and grandfather. And indeed there is no monarchism more fervent than that which looks to the Crown as to the one and only power in the State capable of redressing the inequalities involved in setting sheriff and bishop in authority over the rest of us, and over us nonconformists more than most.

3

On an Arctic shore

My children by the time they are eighteen have lived in two continents and under half a dozen flags. But my world when I was eighteen was the region of South Yorkshire and North Derbyshire that is sometimes called Hallamshire. Any place south of Ashbourne or north of York was then more foreign to me than France or Italy has ever been to my children. The sense of an anchorage, of a home-place, such a consolation to me through my twenties even, is something I have denied to them. So how can they understand what it meant for me to move south to Cambridge, and then a year later southward again, when I reported to join the Navy at Fareham outside Portsmouth? At last I was securely in manorial England, the only *real* England – if reality is measured and underwritten, as I thought and still think it is, by the records of the imagination! A few years ago I put this into a poem called 'Hampshire', thinking it of anthropological value at least to have it recorded that in the middle of the twentieth century the two cultures inside England could still be experienced so vividly as indeed at almost all points distinct. But either the poem was misunderstood, or else the point of it was thought to be too trivial to be worth making. And anyhow, who outside England thinks any longer that the making of a point is what a poem can or should be concerned with?

At any rate, once I was in the Navy, my world, simply my experience of geography, exploded outwards very fast. And after I had finished training and reported to my depot at Chatham, the draft-chit that I picked up Read: 'S B N O N R' – Senior British Naval Officer, North Russia.

The passage took four days, on a fast destroyer, the *Blankney*. In Iceland, at Seydisfjord, the snow-capped heights threw long black shadows in the chilly afternoon. The upper deck swayed in a burning sun at midnight, and I lay upon banked hammocks, not daring to move, fighting sea-sickness. We kept watches in the wireless-cabin. Mine was an unimportant and silent frequency, and I read *The Mayor of Casterbridge*. Then the landfall came. The Murman coast rose tawny and bare. The effect in summer sunlight was baked and torrid, Tunisia more than the Arctic Circle.

We landed on the jetty at Polyarno about half-past six in the evening, and we stayed there, sitting on our kit-bags. *Marne* was already alongside, and a big Russian destroyer, the *Grozny*, was moored further along to our left. In the rosy sunshine, the Russian ratings from *Grozny* had rigged a small high net across the jetty and were playing volley-ball. Other sailors strolled up and down, and a lean cropped girl went with one of them. All the Russian sailors, whether in walking-out dress or not, looked clean and smart. Many wore their hair cropped close. *Grozny*, too, shone like a new pin. There was some bartering by signs (though strangely noisy too) over the sides of *Marne*, and we joined in this, with some embarrassment and little success. British cigarettes went one way over the rail, and red-star brooches, bearing a hammer and sickle, went back.

An island cast its big shadow across the water and over us. The mainland rose steeply and curved round into two horns, high cliffs, where it almost met the extremities of the island to make two narrow passages of water, leading to the open sound. The horn on our left, as we looked inland, was nearer and higher. We saw now that the land was not quite bare but covered with low tough bushes. Just below this heathy bluff, and still high above the anchorage, was a building of white stone round three sides of a square. This, we would find out, was the barracks for the submarine-crews when ashore, and the principal Red Fleet establishment in the place. Below this again, a colony of small wooden sheds, with an occasional stone building, trailed over a last big knoll down to the level of the waterfront, round what looked in the distance like flights of wooden steps. From there the waterfront, the wooden jetty, ran almost straight towards us, through a rough barricade about halfway along, where a naval sentry stood. Along the shoreward side of the jetty was a broken line of timber sheds, go-downs, naval storehouses and workshops. Behind that again there was just room for a narrow road under rocky cliffs; these closed our horizon, though there was here and there the hint of a low wooden roof beyond and on top. This road came clearly into view just in front of us, only a few yards away, where was an open way from the jetty to the road. This open space was the focus of all New Polyarno, and there was a good deal of going to and fro across it beside a square pagoda-like Customs House. Beyond the road at this point the cliffs were interrupted by elaborate flights of stone steps, connected with a row of quite imposing buildings, four or five storeys high. A white ensign floated over one of them. The road curled up, round, and out of sight to the right, for there a long dry reach ran inland, broad and steepsided. The jetty finished a few yards off to our right, and beyond the broad reach a long high ridge ran out to the other horn of the curve. Small wooden houses, sparse on that hillside, looked like chalets.

We loaded our kit at last on to a lorry that came, climbed up after it ourselves, and bumped away on the road under the cliffs. Russian 'wrens', small dumpy figures in blue skirts and tunics, with sailor-collars, giggled and waved their hands.

It must have been next morning that we went to Navy House, where we had seen the ensign fly, and were given our duties. Navy House contained the wardroom, and the offices for operations, signals, accountancy, intelligence, liaison. On the top floor was the wireless-receiving room, and quarters for a few ratings. The other ratings, including me, were housed in the Submarine Base.

There were also two outposts. Behind Navy House the hill sloped up steeply, built over with some quite large though dilapidated houses, and some wretched wooden cabins. On a patch of ground in front of one of the large houses still stood a pair of dirty large umbrellas, once gaily coloured, of the sort that shade café-tables, relics perhaps of a time when Polyarno was a summer resort for Murmansk. Unmade roads ran between the rows of stucco houses, and paths wound upwards by the cabins, where occasionally a hard-faced housewife stooped and poked. There was a flight of wooden steps. All these paths and ways led eventually to the transmitting-station, on the top of the hill. This was the first outpost, and when I reached it I had gone through all there was of New Polyarno. At the transmitting-station the buildings stopped, and one looked towards Murmansk over one steep small hill after another, all covered now with ling and shrubs where there was shallow peaty soil; but there was no soil at all on any exposed ground, and what one saw at a glance was the iron-grey of bare rock. On the first of these hills was Y Cottage, the other outpost, which housed a petty-officer and a handful of naval ratings.

I divided my time between the transmitting-station and the receiving-room, and soon learned to feel redundant. Sometimes I was allowed to man a watch on a receiver. More often I did odd jobs, holding on to halyards while others adjusted dipole aerials, sweeping the rocks clear of wood-shavings, or 'loafing' batteries and accumulators up and down the hill, in the uninterrupted golden sunlight of an Arctic July. The weather was as warm as an English summer, and predictable.

Len, cat-like and swarthy, a practised operator, bantered and japed on watch. I choked, appreciative. Such a world of assurance! Such rapid and devious idiom! 'More rabbits than that . . .', 'Good hand in a four-ale bar . . .' And 'barrack-stanchions . . .'

The only centre of amenities was the Red Fleet Club, well-appointed and large. There was a range of upstairs rooms which were closed to us, but we had the run of a spacious hall, a cinema-theatre, a games-room and a swimming bath (though this last, I think, was not always in commission). The hall was hung with photographs, technically fine, and propagandist in intention. One showed British ratings walking on the waterfront, over a caption invoking unshakeable union. About once a week there were dances, to a rapid 'oompah–oompah' from a military band. It was over-heated, and scents hung upon the air.

After a few weeks four new hands were sent out to Y Cottage, and I was one of them. It was a mixed blessing. R.N. chefs worked in Navy House, and a Russian staff cooked and waited at table in the Submarine Base, but Y Cottage was self-supporting, and in periods off watch we cooked, cleaned, repaired, and provisioned ourselves. But we were never worried about discipline, and our time was so full that we seldom saw ratings from the other establishments, so we felt loyal to our own little community. My time at Y Cottage was the best I had until I went to Archangel.

And it was still summer. Summer meant the never-setting sun. As if we were all angels, we walked in what should have been evening, but with the sun like a red lamp still hanging over the islands it seemed eternity. I rose at night and went out of the shuttered cabin, to find the sun still blazing on the rocks and the whinberry bushes. In the mornings I walked about, applauding a world refreshed; and then recalled that it was not, as I was, just waking. The world turned round no more. It hung there, stopped by a finger. In the ruddy evenings, if I went downhill, man-dolines were playing from the honeycombed houses; the music was mournful, unearthly.

There were ten of us now at Y Cottage, and one more came in from the transmitting-station for his meals. He was Eddie Dwyer (the name was assumed), an Alsatian who had served with the French Navy, transferred to the Royal Navy at the fall of France, come ashore in North Russia as a survivor off the cruiser *Edinburgh*, and volunteered to stay. He had only survivor's kit, and looked bigger than he really was, in a Russian felt-lined cap with ear-flaps, and a big lined coat. At meals he talked a great deal, loud and fluently, with his peculiar cadences, sometimes stumbling over a word. He laughed too, very loud and high, showing his big teeth. He was sure of himself, capable, rather lazy, salacious, formidable.

Eddie's Russian was serviceable. In time I picked up enough to stumble earnestly among commonplaces when Russians took refuge with us in the air-raid shelters we had scooped out among the rocks. We would greet effusively the Russians who came sometimes to wheedle cigarettes and chocolate, or to see to the ever-failing water-supply, and the laughing hearty little woman-doctor from the hospital just below us, who took our empty bottles for her medicines; and less wholeheartedly we welcomed the Russian boy with his wits about him, who would trade balalaikas, guitars, belts and knives, or the inevitable and innumerable metal badges, for British and American tobacco. But the men who learned fluent Russian were in billets with Russian servants. A few common idioms we knew, and mispronounced them between ourselves as well as in exchanges with Russians. Our exchanges with them were punctuated with nods and gusty laughter, a forced jocularity as of helpful parents when the ice won't thaw at a children's party. In this and in other ways the extraordinary childishness of Service life was for us accentuated to the infantile.

Yet most of us were older men. I was the baby in a family of grown-up babies. Some beards among us made us seem picturesque, but no Royal Navy man could have been deceived for long into thinking us 'pussers' seamen. One of the beards was carefully tended, silky, brown, and roundly cut around a seductive mouth and chin. That was Charlie West, ex-Merchant Navy, with his slim figure, wicked tongue, and eyes of a speedwell-blue. Another beard was large, jet-black, Assyrian, crisply curling, shaggy and luxuriant. That was Alec Cunningham. The third was sandy, rough but sparse, and bluntly pointed. That was Reg Horsley, whom I specially liked. Reg had a pleasant wit, a capacious memory for disreputable jokes, limericks and songs, and a boyish gusto and buoyancy in everything he did. Yet among the others who had known him longer, though they acknowledged him as a good companion, there was a suspicion of constraint, I suspect, because he was slightly better educated. Reg Horsley was called 'the Inspector', because someone, a survivor off the *Edinburgh* I think, once mistook his name for 'Hornleigh'. But who now remembers that Police-Inspector Hornleigh was a hero of radio-shows? The Inspector had been in the Territorials before the war, had served in France in that first winter of 1939–40; he came back before Dunkirk, went with the York and Lancasters to Norway, and was evacuated from Aandalsnes. Invalided out of the Army, he was conscripted into the Navy later.

Some of us Northerners would play 'nipsy', the Yorkshire colliers' version of knurr-and-spell, on the rocks outside the cabin. Sometimes of an evening when the crocks had been washed up, the Inspector would string his balalaika as a uke and strum away, or Charlie would play his mouth-organ, or the P.O. would produce his Russian guitar. And we, lying in the shadowed bunks, with a duffel-coat thrown over us perhaps, and sea-boots propped on the bed-rail casting enormous shadows back along the blankets, would chorus, 'There's a long long trail a-winding', or 'When the beer is on the table I'll be there', or 'Young Roger of Kildare'. But more often some of the middle- and morning-watchmen would be turned in, reading or drowsing; I would be away with a bundle of signals to Navy House; Nobby, the staid and stable man, a man of method, would be at the table in the Recreation Room, writing letters or learning Russian; the P.O. would be visited by the Chief from Navy House, and they would shriek abuse at each other, drink rum, and talk wireless, women, and personalities, for some hours; and Alex, with our Irish stoker Paddy and perhaps some others, would entertain Jock, Alec's Scottish oppo off the *Chiltern*.

Chiltern was the trawler attached to the base, and Jock would come up the Murmansk road nearly every night, ostensibly for a walk, actually, it was apparent, for rum. At first, taking him at his own valuation, we called him romantically 'the mad steward', because of his stories of firing single-handed all *Chiltern*'s light artillery, to join the ack-ack barrage. But he was a liar, I'm afraid. His call-note, recurring every sixty seconds or so, was, 'Wull, I'll tell ye . . .' And he did tell, at length, in trivial and irrelevant detail. One thing only gave purpose and direction to his life. That was rum, and to that everything he touched was ultimately turned. He fiddled about with canvas, and for bottled rum would turn out kit-bags or leather seats, unserviceable ones, for our broken chairs. Alec, who wouldn't soon speak ill of a fellow Scot, admitted in the end that Jock was 'a blathering bastard'.

I imagine going back now, stepping from a boat, an incongruous pleasure-steamer under the iron cliff. I walk up the steps in the languid August weather, laced, I remember, with little ribbons of chill. Here is the yard or passage-way under the hill; a boy who had played for Chelsea was pretty with his foot-work here, and here my oppo later unlatched his skis. There are ways up the hill – by the wooden stairs; by the sand road where cables swagged from the posts like vines; or else by a basement cobbler's, where a boy called Valya took me and lent me skates; or again to the eastward, where Eddie kept a slut.

The first snow fell at the beginning of September, and beautiful days followed, when the sun was low, casting enormous shadows in the thin and chilly air. Many times we took our tin-hats and raced out of Y Cottage, under the masts and over rocks and ling, while the sirens wailed. From a hollow scooped out of a peaty bank we watched two or three aircraft crawling high through the blue sky, among the wooly gun-bursts, over the empty and spectacular hills. At the end of the month a big new draft arrived. Old acquaintances joined me now, and we were moved back together to the Submarine Base.

The Chief P.O. Telegraphist set the tone for us all, sending the impalpable influence of his fanatical efficiency and his bitter tongue from the receiving-room in Navy House. He it was who made us into a rigid hierarchy, in which the man with an extra star on his badge, or an extra

month on the station, was set immeasurably above the raw products of
the training-school, so that we hated ourselves for shaking, as we did, for
fear the Chief's sarcasm should seek us out, or for wondering, as we did,
if we might dare to intervene on the morning watch in a conversation
between the Leading Hand and the Admiralty operator. The new draft,
unemployed and listless, huddled in blankets playing endless games of
crib. I rummaged through a sack from the R.N. War Libraries, and came
up with the two volumes of Martin's *Life of John Clare*. Outside, a wind like
a knife brought flurries of fine snow to ruffle the sand of the square, and
everything was hesitant and suspended, waiting for winter.

Before long, however, came relief. I was ordered to other work, going
down in *Chiltern* to Vaenga to unload wireless gear from the holds of
merchant-ships. The weather now became severe, and we still wasted
time, loafing about the deck for hours on end. Getting up at half-past-five
and aboard *Chiltern* by seven was no joke, with temperatures falling to
twenty degrees below freezing, the decks covered with ice and frozen
snow. *Chiltern* was late every day leaving the jetty, and the six or so of us
passengers would clamber down to the mess-deck to wait for fifteen or
twenty minutes, before the hands climbed out of bunks and hammocks.
They were a queer crowd, sleeping in ribbed Arctic pants and jersey;
dirty, gap-toothed, broken-nosed, their hair a curly tangle or, like the
quiet young Welshman, lank, yellow and silky in his eyes. One could
hardly believe that only the accident of war had thrown them together in
this dirty craft, under their dirty, drinking R.N.R. skipper, his uniform
jacket held together in the rear with a safety-pin, and the ragged gold
braid of his frayed single ring hanging from his arm.

There, on those dark mornings, I sat and read *Candida* and Sholokhov's
Virgin Soil Upturned. Shaw's *Four Pleasant Plays* came from two shelves of
books in the darkest corner of the foc's'le. There was also *The Gentleman
from Indiana* and A. E. W. Mason's *Clementina*, together with Maeter-
linck's *Wisdom and Destiny*. And in that last, as in so many, was a faded
fragrance of forgotten and now inexplicable fly-leaf dedications: 'To
Karin, in remembrance of one of the happiest times of her life, from
Phyllis, June 1916.' Who was Karin? And did she ever expect that her
name would start questions, in a British trawler off the Murman coast?

When we reached our destination, and came alongside a Russian troop-
ship, the sun would be rising. Along the deck above us filed the soldiers,
very young, all of a size, small and stocky, quiet, timid and incurious, all
Central Asian about the eyes. The sunrise might be fine. A ledge of black
cloud would hang low, crowding the sun on the horizon, but there were
dwarf conifers above Vaenga, standing out against the sun, and the snowy
hills west of the inlet changed for half an hour to a faint pink.

Henry was with me on these trips, and in my new billet also. He was an old acquaintance in a way, but I never knew him well until this time. We were not friends even then, except for a few days after the arrival of our October mail. Henry never got much mail. That was not surprising, considering the pains it cost him to write a letter. Such grim ordeals with stubby pencil, such laborious readings aloud, usually to me – letters to his parents, each sentence beginning, 'Well, Mum . . .', to his mate and his brothers, 'Well, boy . . .', to his girl, 'Well, darling . . .' His October mail depressed him, and he set about replying to it at once. The trouble appeared: his younger brother, having just gone to sea, had come home on leave talking portentously of suicide. It had upset his family, obviously. Even his father had written, an unparalleled event – an inarticulate brief note. Henry wrote his brother a letter, pretending to have heard nothing, striking a note of masculine camaraderie. His brother had spent some time in Reform School. 'I thought them schools was reckoned to make a man of you,' he said disgustedly, 'but they made a bloody pansy out of him.' He had a good mind to write about his brother. 'There's a society about such things, isn't there? I'll tell you what. You've had education. You could write that letter.' I never did. He had another brother, younger still, at Reform School now. 'But if they touch my Bobby . . .' 'They' meant the call-up. 'The Old Woman', his mother, had been drinking and offering to fight all the Police Reserve. But that was not a worry. Henry laughed delightedly.

Chiltern would come alongside the British or American merchantman while her decks were being hosed with scalding water to break the ice. So we would hang about until the ice was gone and the hatches could be raised. Then packing-cases were slung out on to the Russian tender on the other side of the ship. Usually it was noon before we were allowed into the hold to scrabble with benumbed fingers for cases with the cypher that declared them wireless equipment. If there were many of these our luck was in and we could get warm hooking them into the slings and swinging them up and out, as the short afternoon drew on. More often we had come for no more than half a dozen cases and we returned to yawning boredom after only thirty minutes' work in the whole day. All the time Henry would be looking for packing-cases broken open, from which he could snatch a can of fruit or a winter vest. He was annoyed with me because I would not co-operate, at least to the extent of hiding what he handed me, in the folds of my duffel-coat. In this way he could force me into a foolish attitude of civic indignation. Really what stopped me was the thought of my mortification if we were caught. Pilfering was as natural to him as self-consciousness to me. To pass the time, we sparred at each other with our leather gauntlets, as *Chiltern* turned her nose for home. A better man than I am, Henry Prior? That's only patronizing upside-down. But by many scales of value he certainly was – notably by the never outmoded values of warfare. I have lived with that knowledge, uncomfortably, ever since.

And again I was suddenly lucky, saved for a spell from barren Polyarno, where the British lived in their private world, sustained by cult and riddled with intrigue. I was posted to Murmansk. I went in a Russian motor-launch up the inlet, extravagantly impressed (as usual) by the unimpressive efficiency of the crew of three, excited by the foreign smell of them, greatly expectant. I knew this could be worse than Polyarno. And stupefied by the desolation of Murmansk's bombed waterfront, I began to see what the worse might be. An officer's politeness, when I reported to British headquarters, alarmed me still more.

But I need not have worried. Malenki Dom, the house on the outskirts to which I was sent, was a community as Y Cottage had been. Also, it was international: a P.O. Telegraphist and three wireless-operators, together with four Russian servants, made a nucleus round which hovered a floating population of D.E.M.S. ratings (naval gunners loaned to merchant ships), soldiers and occasionally airmen. And it was a youthful community. Alec Cunningham and 'Inspector' Horsley had looked upon us youngsters with an avuncular eye whereas here we ran wild by ourselves. For that matter the P.O. at Murmansk could be avuncular too, but only in his professional field. He was young, a slow Norfolk man, with an uncertain temper and inclined to be jittery in air-raids, but with a subdued passion for his job. His was only an auxiliary station, with one transmitter and two receivers, and this suited him, for his heart was in operating more than administration. Atmospheric conditions in the area were consistently bad, and unsurmountable when the Northern Lights were out; and it was an education to see him woo the faintest and most blurred signal out of a raucous tangle of interference, or patiently smooth the answers from his transmitting-key. With just the same careful gentleness he would have us tapping a dead key for practice, flexing the wrist at the right time and to the right angle, while he plied us with assiduous blandishments or infrequent insidious ironies. We took it in turns to assist him with calls through the night, and rather than go to bed between one call-period and the next we would remain at the sets, while he talked slowly of the sand-yacht he had built during a previous commission in Aden. As an N.C.O., he was allowed a monthly spirit-ration and in the early hours was liberal with gin. He did not trouble about discipline off watch, and our rum, which he served us neat, we bottled day by day for a night's drinking at the end of the week. At six o'clock in the morning, gently fuddled after all night at the sets, we greeted Katerina, our cook, who raised her hands with a mournful 'Ai! ai!' at our condition, then served creamy yellow *kasha* for our breakfast. After that we tumbled into our beds until the afternoon.

Snow lay deep and frozen hard by now. To go down to the makeshift 'heads' at the bottom of the garden was as daunting because of the cold as because of the stench. We stirred abroad very seldom. Sonya, burning logs behind an iron plate in the wall, would let the fire die after thirty minutes and would push in the damper, so that the heat was held and circulated inside the double wall of the wooden house, making it wonderfully cosy. My stockinged feet pressed hard against this stove, I read *Lavengro* and *A Sentimental Journey*.

Zoya, our housekeeper, was a very pleasant and capable thirty-two-year-old woman from the Ukraine. She was cheerful and always ready for a joke, taking teasing in good part; so it was a surprise to learn that her husband and child had been killed in the Ukraine (her husband, she suspected, hanged as a locally prominent party-member), both her parents killed, three of her brothers lost at the Front, and finally the family of her only surviving brother, with whom she lived in Murmansk, dead also, I think in an air-raid. Katerina, the chef, an older woman, was charming; she had a punctilious sort of courtesy that I never saw in any other Russian. Her almost inaudible knock on the door was the perfection of modesty and discretion, and she moved around her kitchen, with her fuzzy black hair, in her rusty black dress, a cigarette at an oddly aggressive angle in the inevitable holder, with the demure composure of a well-bred girl at her first ball. Sonya, young and immensely fat, did the heavy work of fires, cleaning, and splitting logs. I tried to split logs for her once, but they were frozen solid, and I watched in mortified silence as Sonya made them fly apart. If one did nothing at all but look at her hard in silence, Sonya's great round face would split into the widest and most infectious of masculine grins and 'O-ho, O-ho' she would trumpet, till one had to laugh with her. 'She is a lovely thing', Harold West would say, staring at her dreamily; and away she would go into shrill guffaws and a flood of incomprehensible Russian. But one morning nothing could raise that grin, and as she made my bed she began to blubber. Her husband, wounded in thigh and hip, after eight months in hospital and two at home, was to return to the front – 'limping', she made me understand, her eyes streaming, 'among the ice and snow'. Two days later she was as hearty as ever. Only of Anna, little, scrubby, insignificant, shrill, was nothing known except – a momentous exception – that she carried tales. There was one of those in every working group.

An air-raid shelter had been made by Harold West and others, some twenty yards behind the house. It was simply a stone dug-out neatly excavated in the side of a bank, and at first we took refuge there whenever the sirens wailed. But we were so near the Finnish lines that often the aircraft was overhead when the warning came. The guns opened up, and we ran as much risk from falling shrapnel if we dashed across the open ground as from the bombs if we stayed indoors. Also, it was a labour, throwing on the clothes necessary in those temperatures. Then again, the enemy made their run-in over us, conserving their bombs for the dock-area or the centre of town. Besides, the period of intensive bombing was over, and at this time it was a matter of one or two aircraft appearing every couple of hours, to drop half a dozen bombs and depart. On the whole it was as well to stay in bed. In fact Murmansk was at a stage when bombing-attacks had only nuisance-value. The damage had been done by incendiary bombs, and standing on the slope above our dug-out we looked over to a whole hillside weirdly diversified by the brick chimney-stacks which alone survived from a suburb of timber houses. Only some office-blocks, hospitals and public buildings in the centre were of stone. Only a crazy shack here and there was left standing in the area of the docks. Yet vessels could still anchor, unload and re-fuel in Kola Sound.

Life in Murmansk was feverish and temporary; the soul of the town had been knocked out and it had reverted to a life raw and unformed, the life of a wild frontier, a mushroom town of the gold rush in the Yukon or California. It was a town of enormous vistas, so much having been demolished, full of the blank shine of beaten snow muted and dimmed under the leaden skies, full of more snow, in always shortening and now sunless days. In the Post Office, where I sent a telegram for my father's birthday, the girls wore fur-coats with big rolled collars in the fashion of the British twenties, and their gloved fingers flew, rattling the battered beads along the frame of the abacus that stood by every counter. All Russian customers save the young seemed as mystified as I was, though whining and blustering outside the grilles. As I went home squads of soldiers stamped in long coats, singing solemn martial songs in perfect time, their faces set and expressionless. Some sleighs, raised on curved runners, spun magnificently behind trotting horses. More were heavy and laden, driven by fierce bearded men in many ragged furs. Were these farmers from the wastes behind the town? A walk to Kola showed me homesteads, but how could one farm in this climate? Everything merged, shone an instant and fell back in the perpetual twilight. The snow deadened every sound.

I returned to Polyarno on Christmas Eve, clambering over *Bramble* and *Gleaner*, moored alongside. The first was a corvette, the second a fleet-sweeper. Two or three such smaller vessels remained in Russian waters from one convoy to the next, sweeping the inlet or running stores from Polyarno to Archangel and back. It was a week later that *Bramble* vanished for good in the Northern mists, without so much as a cheep from her radio.

There was a deceptive warmth of welcome from old mess-mates, in the huge dank wash-house at the Submarine Base. But really Polyarno was as ever. Drink flowed freely that Christmas Eve, and under the stress of new resolutions I made the mistake of abstaining. Even drink brought no good fellowship here. One rowdy drunk put his foot through my balalaika that was scrawled with signatures Russian and English, and another, maudlin, told me tearfully of his grandmother when I supported him on watch at midnight. Next day was remarkable only for a thaw, of all unlikely things. And in the evening a carol-singing party in the Navy House wardroom degenerated within an hour to a babel of bawdry.

A week later, on New Year's Day, I kept the forenoon watch. In the warm stale air, on my neglected frequency, I yawned and fidgeted. But the Port Wave operator, leaning back on his stool and chatting, stiffened suddenly, called out, and feverishly wooed his set. The Leading Hand looked over the operator's shoulder, gasped, and shot out of the room. Remote dignitaries like the Flag-Lieutenant appeared, and on every bay but mine the operator broke traffic and began to beat his transmitting-key. *Onslow*, leading the outward-bound convoy's escort, was reporting sighting the German task-force: 'One battleship, one cruiser, so many destroyers . . .' *Tirpitz* was out of her fiord at last, and *Hipper* with her. 'Am engaging', said *Onslow*, and fell silent. After that, only rumours – notably, that we had requested Soviet air-support, which came too late and too sparingly. *Onslow* had limped into Murmansk, and her dead and wounded had been landed at Vaenga, before we knew that Captain Sherbrooke had indeed led his destroyers against the battleship, and that the German force had broken off the engagement.

And so for a time Polyarno was populous with visiting ships. The personnel of the British base put on a concert, where Henry and I met an acquaintance off *Obedient*, and one Sunday I saw a familiar face in the throng crowding out of a cinema show in the Fleet Club. It was Duncan Harrigan, charming irredeemable 'skate' of my training-class, who used to bring me bannocks from his leaves in Paisley. He had been twice torpedoed in the nine months since I had known him in Fareham.

But before long we had to be self-sufficient again. There was bad feeling in the Submarine Base, where we were broken up into cliques. Some of these were closed to me automatically: such was, for instance, the company of three or four seamen who jealously guarded the quantities of drink and victuals they had pilfered from the stores, of which they prepared gargantuan meals at all hours of the day. Others were unexciting: Nobby Clarke and his oldish bourgeois friends, with their tennis-club jokes and rubbers of bridge. What with my natural timidity, and a confused sense that I should get beyond the limitations of my background and my class, I gravitated towards the most disreputable community of all, where Henry from his bed in the corner, surrounded by stacks of pilfered clothing, presided over 'the skates', rowdy, insubordinate, inquisitive about the Russians, full of salty humour. One petty-officer, I remember, took me to task for lending the support of my education to the worst element in the place. But to join the side of law and order seemed to mean being only half-alive, living in Arctic Russia as if one were still in Streatham or Stockport. Henry and his friends were alive, open to new impressions, flexible. This was true not only of Henry himself but of Freddy Burke's less instinctive, more passionate denial of authority, and even, though with a difference, of Charlie, a member of the gang even more strangely incompatible, apparently, than I was. Charlie was forty-ish, a bachelor, bald and small, with a strange dry cackle of a laugh. He had been with the same firm in the City for twenty years. That, one would have thought, should have taught him docility enough. It had; and he would never see that the restrictions which had hedged him round as a junior clerk were, though different, hardly less than those he endured as a coder. Charlie's kind of rebellion was comically illustrated by a story which he told with pride one forenoon: he had kept the morning watch in Navy House, and went into the mess there to eat his breakfast. This was improper, though generally winked at, and a petty-officer, noticing Charlie, would have sent him packing with 'No grub here for a Submarine Base rating!' 'Don't you call me a rating!' flared Charlie, trembling through all his five feet six. Henry treated him with affectionate mockery, the point of which was lost on him. 'Ain't he a boy?' Henry would appeal, bemused in pretended awe at some tiny insubordination. And Charlie would bridle, with a secret smile. Later I remember him trying to match our indecencies with anecdotes of a shady cabaret on a Mediterranean cruise he had taken before the war.

Although this group was more open towards the Russians, there was little chance for this to show itself. When the chance came, it came from outside Polyarno, only to be nipped in the bud. Two Canadian ratings appeared in the room which five or six of us shared. They had crossed the Atlantic in a Russian submarine, managing signals liaison with allied vessels along the way. They had not been with us many days before they were visited by Russians who had been their shipmates. We were glad and excited, and a party was arranged. The Russians, used to eating 'zakouski' (snacks) with their vodka, demanded and got great hunks of bread and jam to go with the rum we gave them. They were very ill. A couple of them called again more than once, but were never at ease. We knew why. A Russian, a commissioned interpreter, was being entertained by the P.O.s at the other end of the corridor, while Georgi and his friend were with us. The pleasantest of our Chief P.O.s, just slightly 'lit up', suddenly appeared in our room in the Russian's peaked cap and epauletted greatcoat. Nothing we could say would hold our friends after that. For a long while after, a Russian N.C.O. would suddenly enter almost every evening, to stare in silence round our room, then bow and depart. We pretended he was there to check on the black-out curtains. After that our only Russian visitor prepared to break what was evidently a ban on fraternizing was one whom we called Fidoto. He had close-cropped hair, a comical high-pitched laugh, a big loosely jointed frame, and a lop-sided slouch. The close crop, he said, was a penalty for over-stopping shore-leave, I think in Panama. His was a temperament that might in an earlier age have been called typically Russian, for he had few of the domestic virtues and all the attractive social ones. He was a good companion, played on his balalaika a passable imitation of American 'swing', and left us most nights rather the worse for rum. His amused disregard for authority impressed us by contrast to our other guests' anxieties. And he was no simple 'skate'. He talked of Turgenev and Gorky, but also of Walter Scott, Byron, Charlotte Brontë. One midday when he came he had under his arm an *Iliad* in translation.

Now the weather turned really fierce. For day after leaden day snow fell thickly through the gloom, until every so often a furious wind, rising too soon for the moored ships to sheer off into open water, would whirl the flakes into a blizzard that damaged the ships by dashing them against the jetty. For Henry and myself short spells of operating alternated with long intervals when we were wiremen, tramping the iron hills with a ladder between us, and fumbling with gloved hands at the leaning posts which sometimes carried as many as half a dozen power cables slung above the frozen earth. Henry was more useful and efficient than I was, climbing the masts with irons on his feet, while the snow whirled round his clumsy bulk perched dizzily above me. We had been issued with unsuitable clothing, immense conical hats with seal-skin ear-flaps, and wool-lined leather coats, extremely heavy and hot, long-skirted, and soon frozen stiff as a board. The luckier ones, like Freddy Burke, had secured a Russian 'shuba'. In the evenings Henry and the skates went slut-hunting, which meant going round the Russian dwellings and entering, on any pretext or none at all, any room that struck the fancy. The Russians responded, apparently, with courtesy and restraint.

And still luck ran my way. For pat, in April, came a draft-chit for Archangel. Three of us got the draft, and were much envied. To the ratings at Polyarno. Archangel was a promised land; life was easier there, one heard of hugely profitable rackets in NAAFI rations, there was an abundance of drink. Above all, there were women. And yet I felt misgivings. Life there, by all accounts, was strange, hectic and violent. And large figures from Conrad and Kipling, of Englishmen gone to the bad abroad, stalked in my thoughts through the tales of wild parties, of kept mistresses, of prodigious drunks. Literature still was grease paint and footlights to life.

4

Closing a chapter

It was in April of 1943 that we sailed from Polyarno for Archangel, three of us, in S.S. *Bering*, an American merchantman proceeding in a small convoy of eight ships, British, American and Russian. We messed with the American gunners, and we worked our passage by assisting the solitary signalman. Apprehensive at first of my ability to read Morse lamp, I was proud of a new accomplishment after two days' practice. We ate sumptuously; each meal was a revelation, and I remember particularly mountainous breakfasts, sweet corn and mugs of fragrant coffee. Many of the merchant-seamen were British, and some of the younger deck-hands, as well as the Yankee gunners, would join us in our cabuche for'ard, properly the sick-bay, to ask us about life ashore. The fifteen-year-old cabin-boy, who was British or Canadian (I forget which), was especially friendly. I admired his courage, for he had run away from home to join the ship, but my admiration had a bad taste to it, for he had 'got a dose'. The admiring jocularity of his older mess-mates showed how he had had to prove himself a man. Another of that group in the sick-bay, a young Welshman, was in the same state when I met him, a month later, in an Archangel street; yellowed, beaded with sweat.

I remember from the trip the affectations of the Americans, and a passage through fragmentary pack-ice at the mouth of the Dvina. 'Affectations' is wrong; what fascinated me in the Americans was a whole system of muscular notation which I got to know later in the acting of Humphrey Bogart, a range of mannerisms which built up to an impression of languid power. It was exciting to watch the way they walked, shrugged on their clothes, or lit a cigarette. There was nothing of the sort with the Russians, and I never felt with them the powerful foreignness of these Americans.

We were bound for Molotovsk, a sprawling vigorous new port at the Dvina mouth. At the edge of the ice we kept a rendezvous with two big Soviet ice-breakers, but little ice was left and that was broken up; so I stood in the bows, in a damp pearly mist that had suddenly come upon the ships, hearing the thrust of the engines, interrupted by a swish and crunch as the bows met a slab of ice, and the long painful grind as the slab rocked and brushed along the sides.

More even than Murmansk or Polyarno, Molotovsk was a frontier town. My fancy placed it north and east, on the fringes of undeveloped Siberia where the places had names like Dickson, as in the Wild West. Long columns of workers, men and women, were marched about in their quilted jackets, inmates of the labour-camps. Beside them swarmed sailors of many nations, and Red Army soldiers. Already here the snow was disappearing, but if it had lain thick the town would still have looked raw and unfinished. Its low wooden buildings sprawled, beside wide roads hardly distinguishable from waste lots where a post leaned awry, where piles of stones and wooden billets had been abandoned haphazard.

Ice was coming down the Dvina, and mingled with great fleets of floating logs, when we waited on the waterfront at Bakharitsa, staring across the big river at the roofs of Archangel. About thirty Poles waited on the jetty, desperate and ragged, one detachment of the caravans then roaming from Siberia to the Persian Gulf, prisoners one day, disbanded soldiers the next, unwanted always. This was just after Sikorski's note on the alleged massacre of Polish officers near Smolensk. Russian feeling against the Poles was more than usually hostile. 'What, are we dogs then?' cried a Pole to a Russian sentry who would have moved them on so that they should not speak to us. They wanted to speak. 'Englishmen!' – they looked at us as if we were gods, come down from the longed-for skies. We told them of the Polish army in Scotland, and I had an incongruous vision of a party of Polish officers, eyeglassed and fleshy exquisites, in a railway dining-room at Perth when we had passed through for Thurso and Scapa. One of our party, a signalman, had six months before evacuated Polish women and children to East Africa, from a port in Persia.

Our quarters in Archangel were luxurious by the standards we were used to in Polyarno, and at first I had little work to do. I wandered about the streets. A long main thoroughfare, Prospekt Vinogradski, followed the course of the Dvina, one block inland from the waterfront. It ran from a new industrial area, of saw-mills and logging yards, downstream past the blasted facade of the University. Gutted in one of two heavy air-raids the year before, the University was still, behind its statue of Lomonosov, impressive in a melancholy way. Reaching the centre of the city at a crossroads beside the Intourist hotel, and near the 'International Club', Prospekt Vinogradski grew noisy with rattling coupled trams, and was bordered for the next mile by buildings of stone and brick, not timber. Most of these were big shops and department stores, many now boarded up, all fly-blown. The finest moment came with the Bolshoi Theatre on the left, big and impressive, decently built in red brick, in the centre of a patch of park. After the theatre, the big block of the Sovietski Dom, the City Hall, was shabby and pretentious. Then came the slick little Victory

Cinema, a concrete cube, where I was to see, with significant omissions, a dubbed version of the movie 'Mission to Moscow'. And at last, after more office-blocks, the timber houses reappeared opposite the tree-lined walks of the Dynamo Stadium. Prospekt Vinogradski ran on as far as a bridge of boats to Salombala, a port new-built by convict labour on an island below the city.

But I preferred the streets behind Vinogradski. Here, in a profusion of green trees, streets of timber sleepers ran between wooden houses, and there was no sound of trams or motor traffic. There was soft singing and strumming, on the summer evenings I remember, white figures flitting against dark timber, and fowls and cattle rooting by the side of streams under the roadway. There was water always beneath one's feet, for the sidewalks were of timber also, often above the level of the roads, and quite often a sleeper became unpinned at both ends, so that as one stepped on it, it would fling up its far end and submerge with a splash into the marsh. There were smells, and many of the houses were settling at odd angles. Some of them, the older houses, were beautiful with carvings in ingenious panels, with a sort of dog-tooth design on lintels, with scroll-work at the base of the beams. Only at each end of these Prospekts did the houses give way to long communal barracks. But the houses too held several families apiece.

There was a great difference, in tone and feeling, between the two stations, Polyarno and Archangel. The year was further advanced here, spring was in the air, and so I saw the difference at first as altogether and brilliantly to the credit of Archangel. No invisible wall existed here between Russian town and British colony. We were quartered in a Russian house, and we moved freely in and out, with no showing of passes nor challenging from sentries. A staff of nearly a dozen Russian women were in the house with us. They slept elsewhere, and were officially our servants. But the younger ones flirted and ragged with us, and the older women mothered us as they had in Murmansk, but more intensely because the population of Karl Marx House was more stable than that of Malenki Dom. Our dear Natasha, for instance, wept copiously each time a draft left for home. Almost every man had his *barishna*, his girl-friend, and not all of these were sluts of the waterfront; some were self-respecting and charming girls, who introduced their English sailors to their families. But there was a bad taste to Archangel, the longer I stayed there. As merchantmen swung at anchor in the river all through that summer of 1943, waiting for a convoy escort that did not come, there were growing queues of syphilitic seamen outside a British Army sick-bay opposite the Dynamo, and a smell of stale sweat hung around the rooms of the International Club. There was pathos in the abandoned mistresses

51

of departed Englishmen, who hung about, branded in Russian eyes, in the road before Karl Marx House, then suddenly disappeared.

The ladies who helped at the International Club were disconcertingly familiar. They could have appeared in the uniform of the W.V.S. without starting a suspicion in any British street; I expected to see under their arms books from Boots Lending Library. They were, in the first place, so definitely 'ladies'; their manners were suburban. In fact I never decided what, in Soviet terms, their environment could be. They represented obviously a provincial intelligentsia. But what their homes were, how much money they had, how they got married and died, whether they were Christian . . . I reproach myself now for my laziness, but at the time it seems I was not aware of these questions, and never in a way to answer them. Chiefly I felt with them, as with their British counterparts, an unbridgeable discrepancy between the entertainment they had to offer, and the needs and preoccupations of their visitors. Their approach was civilized and much forgiving; our response was brutal and boorish, and could not have been anything else.

My own response was no exception. One of the younger ladies, having held me in conversation in the central room, restlessly decorated with photographs, flags, slogans and huge cardboard heads of Stalin, Churchill and Roosevelt, invited me to the first rehearsal of a play to be done in English by British males and Russian ladies. I went to about three rehearsals. I was given a principal part, and on those first occasions we worked roughly through the play. It was when the play stood revealed in all its ungainly length, that I lost nerve and fled. I put them to much trouble, for I was not brave enough to lie myself out of the commitment; I merely stayed away. But I had to get out of it. It had to do with a tank's crew of Red Army soldiers, and their relations with the girls at home who sent them parcels. All the characters were unnaturally boisterous, with a humourless gaiety that slid frequently into long and unexceptionable declarations of brassy patriotism, compared with which the most wooden of British propaganda-plays – say, Priestley's appalling *How Are They At Home?* – were inexpressibly subtle, complex and alive. Casting about for an analogy, I could think only of serial stories in a Baptist magazine that came into the house when I was a schoolboy. Only there could I recall anything strangled so surely by its own rectitude. Productions no better marred the otherwise admirable season of operettas and peasant-concerts at the Bolshoi Theatre.

I remember that one of the other principal parts was taken by an officer new to the station, uncritically enthusiastic about all things Russian, painstakingly exact and therefore far from fluent in his learning of the language, efficient and pedantic at his job, and deservedly unpopular.

One must reserve a special dislike for such as him – there is at least one in every establishment, naval or academic or whatever – because they have all the appearance of energetic sympathy with none of the reality. His views were as rigid and irrational, as unmodified by anything he saw and heard, as the views of those who hated him, who foamed at the mouth every time a Russian appeared. Yet such as he, the exact, of the affable and inhuman smile, were the only men to whom the advances of the lady-interpreters could mean anything at all. And the ladies deserved something better. For they had courage, as I realize now, visualizing one elderly lady nodding and tripping round a circle of ruffian seamen and their painted drabs, inviting them to join her in a peasant dance.

After this piece of cowardice I avoided the ladies at the Club. They were still kind, however, though baffled and sometimes reproachful about my defection. I had resumed reading the Russian novels, in translation from the Club library, and sometimes I would draw one of the ladies into discussing what I had lately read. Her enthusiasm was always boundless. But it was also evasive, and these conversations were comically self-conscious on both sides, a sort of formal encounter, joined in the sacred name of *kultura*, in which the names of Pushkin, Scott, Sholokhov, Jack London were racqueted to and fro like tennis-balls. A shrewdly placed shot could get my opponent into difficulties. Dostoievsky was a back-hand drive. He was approved of course – was he not a classic? – but immediately soft-pedalled, and finally dismissed with the damning epithet, 'morbid'. The judgments and preferences expressed were always the same: Turgenev for instance was always 'the stylist'.

All Russian women were sure that they had equal chances with men of becoming doctors, lawyers, engineers and commissars – also of serving before the mast, clearing the streets of snow in the depth of an Arctic winter, sawing and hauling logs. They had been told, and were sure, that to an Englishwoman all professions were closed. Two years of Land Girls at home had taken the edge off my surprise at finding women in Russia doing heavy labour. Indeed the pattern of social life, as I observed it in Archangel, was in many ways surprisingly familiar. There as at home girls linked arms and roamed in groups in the evenings, making eyes at prospective escorts. There as at home they were conductors in the trams, they served in shops, worked as stenographers, postwomen and clerks. The magnificently developed young women who lay around the Bolshoi on Sunday afternoons, cuddling rifles, or at the Dynamo ground jabbed perfunctorily with bayonets at swinging sacks, seemed not to take the business much more seriously than the children of nine or ten who paraded and drilled with wooden toy rifles in the playgrounds of the schools. Sometimes the familiarity was startling. A girl of twenty was sorry she had had to leave school at thirteen because her father had died about that time and there had not been enough money in the house. She talked wistfully of how as a little girl she had gone with her father, salmon-fishing in the Dvina; and she seemed to be holding fast by a tradition of yeoman independence, personal privacy, family loyalty. Apart from anything else, she was a Christian, and told me there were two churches open in Archangel, at opposite ends of the town. In the village where she was born she had lived, she said, in 'a big house'; and since her move to Archangel, and her reduced circumstances, seemed to date from about 1930, I supposed she belonged to one of the *kulak* families liquidated about that time. She did not deny this, but only said that her father had prospered by his own efforts, not by hiring the labour of others. She never complained of her life, and was enthusiastically proud of the Red Army. She was naturally gay and warm-hearted, though despondent, when I knew her first, over a British sweetheart lately departed. A Stakhanovite, she had one of the best jobs in her trade in Archangel, tending for us. And life could be pleasant for her, wandering on those sunlit evenings through the insanitary but picturesque and grass-grown streets, to boating or swimming parties on the Dvina, or dancing in the open air on the crowded dance-floor of the Dynamo. For the summer nights of never-setting suns were different here from in Polyarno; not out of time but deeply in it, immemorial. Archangel was Old Russia, not a frontier-town.

The blue caps and facings of the police, the *militzia*, were at every corner, and parading the streets as well. It was when I came off the middle watch at four o'clock in the morning, walking through the beaming streets back to Karl Marx House, that I realized how many of them were posted up and down the sleeping city. Few of the men and girls of the *militzia* had the jack-in-office arrogance of the Storm Trooper. With the ubiquitous urchins who clambered on the roofs and couplings of the moving trams, or traded with us foreigners for cigarettes and chocolate, the *militzia* seemed mostly ineffectual.

Despite the war, Russian life was not grim. Laughter and songs, especially songs, were always in the air. Even the quite rare ardent and bigoted nationalists forgot themselves in riotous horse-play. There was one evening at a circus when one of them, a charming though arrogant girl, enthused over Russian physique and strength, and the broken-down old toughs who wrestled before us in the circus-ring – 'You haven't any men like that.' The gaiety was genuine. Yet with it went also the habit of striking a pose. 'There is always the river', they would declare wildly; and perhaps they meant it.

The girl at the circus was Lyuba, and the girl who had gone salmon-fishing was Granya. They were friends. I came to Archangel with a love-letter to Granya from her former sweetheart. He had called in Polyarno on his way home, a pasty sedate young married man, who gave me the letter in the clammy mist of approaching thaw, on a board-walk below the transmitting-station. Lyuba excited me more, at first. Her body was magnificent, statuesque and athletic, beautifully proportioned on a grand and opulent scale, very strange and attractive to English eyes. She was well-educated, a schoolmistress. But she was very unpredictable. Granya told me that Lyuba's father was Siberian, not Russian. And there was certainly something about her that I thought of as primitive. She was fiercely puritan about cosmetics and flirtations. She never dallied with any men, British or Russian, and once, when I had taken the pair of them to dance at the International Club, and I tried to take a kiss, she rebuffed me with embarrassed laughter but a dangerous gleam in her eyes. The gleam appeared at other times, when it did her less credit. She took offence very easily, making no allowance for instance for my stumbling Russian. Then she would stalk away in a fit of fiery sulks that lasted for days. When she was in good humour she would be often laughing, and quite overpoweringly cheerful. And yet she was altogether humourless, and could never take a joke. I see her now, laughing and magnificent, a can of sugared beer in one hand, a raw fish in the other.

Granya was more civilized. She was small and slim. There, in her trimness and daintiness, was her attraction for an Englishman, and she made the most of it, being vivacious where other Russian women were statuesque. Her features were too strong for beauty, but she made up for this with a clear complexion and a distinctive crooked smile. I would stay in the mess alone, struggling slowly round the dart-board on doubles, hearing her laugh in the kitchen, waiting for her to emerge.

Early that summer I went to her birthday party, in a room that her elder sister had in Salombala. Deciding to defy the curfew despite the blazing sunlight, I dodged home at three in the morning along the waterfront, dashing across the intersections when the backs were turned of the armed *militzia*-girls a block away. It must have been August before Granya took me to her more permanent home, a room rented by her other married sister, Shura, in a communal dwelling-house at the other end of Archangel. There I looked through the family photographs. In one family group of 1918, browned and curling at the edges, the father, a partriarchal figure with an impressive curling beard and uncompromising brows beneath a high forehead, held a small child in one half of the picture, while a stiff dim figure, his wife, held another baby on her knee opposite him. A large family of all ages postured around them. It was a trio of dashing young blades in the background, all flowing ties and rakish boaters, and a small boy in a sailor-suit like a board, black stockings drawn over knees, that recalled my own family records, my grandfather posed in broadcloth at the door of a Dorset cottage, and an alien father photographed in boyhood and in youth, in and out of khaki.

Now the mother had returned to the original village and there, old and failing, she lived with an unmarried daughter. I met her several times when she came on a visit. Granya was always excited at the prospect, and greeted her with rapture. But after the first welcoming she was ignored, sitting in a corner crooning mournfully to herself, sometimes tearful. Also in the village was a daughter-in-law whom I never saw. She had two or three children, and their father had been reported lost at the Front. The family was anxious for news of a younger boy, feared lost at sea. But I was there when this brother suddenly appeared in the doorway, and all his sisters cast themselves on his neck. He had been stranded by the ice at Dickson Island, in the far north. From Shura's husband too no mail had arrived in months. That proved nothing, for the postal service from the Army was capricious to say the least. Shura worried, struggling with a sewing-machine to maintain herself and her six-year-old Rima. Katya, the youngest girl, was conscripted into the Army while I was there, but reappeared mysteriously in a matter of weeks, her fair hair cut attractively short, having apparently travelled no further than to Vologda. She was a worry, having taken up with a boy whom the family did not approve. He was a soldier with a shaven head, in hospital blue. In September dusks he and she would lie on the floor, locked in intimate embrace, while Granya and Shura and Rima and I stepped around them and over them. There was talk of some of the younger generation moving to the Ukraine after the war, and they tried to keep together by family gatherings for festivals and name-days. The children were trained and cared for, not allowed to run begging and thieving about the streets, and Granya and her sisters fought for personal and domestic cleanliness in a hopeless struggle against small rooms in overcrowded and verminous timber-houses. I see Rima, late at night, rush into the room terrified by a rat she had seen in the corridor; Granya, clasping her niece in her arms, turning to me where we sat on the stove, blinded with tears of humiliation and disgust. I see the pair of us standing on the porch, and a woman from one of the other rooms rushing out from a party to relieve herself before our eyes upon the snow, and Granya, ugly again with humiliation – 'That we should have to live with such people . . .' I was soon implicated very deeply in the life of this family. But other images I have, of Granya at her name-day party in Salombala lacing her boots for a peasant dance, of Granya and me returning in a tiny motorboat from the island in the Dvina that was just like an English wood, masses of elder-bloom foaming over the gunwales

– these belong to another Granya, a gay coquette with a sharp tongue.

In Archangel I began to respect level-headedness. In Archangel the men who kept their heads were few, an admirable élite. I was not one of them. Granya prevented that. And I suppose the girl-friends, more than anything else in our life, produced that hysterical atmosphere in which individual character swelled to more than life-size, flared in ever deeper and more startling colours, so that the quietest and dullest of Englishmen became something Byronic and awful. It was still true that the wildly drinking, absurdly infatuated Englishmen who penetrated into Russian homes learned more of Russia than the ironical and detached observers. But the eccentricities which flowered suddenly in unexpected people were very strange and often discreditable by any standards, Russian or English. There was 'X' for instance, the licensed oddity, deliberately uncleanly, inefficient, conscientiously gross (belching immensely from his dirty face). An Oxford graduate, he rose at six for two hours' Greek before breakfast, read Livy in the turmoil of the recreation room, and compiled interminable Russian word-lists. He made great ado with an affectation of 'going native', and I thought this was limited to his grossness and his pedantry about the language until one evening I came upon him most improbably, locked in the arms of a respectable Russian woman. Somewhere behind his hectoring responses to the gibes of the mess – he gave as good as he got – lay a peculiarly arid Christianty, and a theory of historical interpretation by biblical prophecy. His only companion in these mysteries was 'Y', with whom, on a long evenings, he read. Murmurs of Armageddon and the lost tribes drifted from 'Y's bed, where 'Y', his face clenched, listened unhappily. 'Y' was a different case. Big and clean, he kept himself fit, and played any sport with a neat and furious competence. Otherwise he never stirred abroad, except to go on watch, and as the months passed the rage and fear grew behind his eyes whenever the Russians were discussed. Very young, he had joined the Navy from his public-school, and his sixth-form piety must have consorted oddly with the malignant pictures of his companion. But he grasped feverishly at whatever was tinily familiar in this whirl of what was strange, and his homesickness was both painful and secret. The strain which told on him emerged sickeningly one evening when the surface of his good breeding broke for good and all, and he raged amazingly round the room, at all things Russian. The occasion of that outburst was the presentation of a bunch of flowers, by the captain of a Russian football team, to his British opponent. The oddity of that, connected too with sport, that in him which had been most sacred, was apparently more than 'Y' could bear.

Then there was Harry, rotten with drink, radiating dignity from his bed in the corner. An older man; but who, seeing that purple face and sagging figure, would care to say how old he was? Harry was cultured, and spoke Russian well. He was a journalist in civilian life, and there was some question, since it was said that he'd been asked to leave the country when a Moscow correspondent in peacetime, whether he should have been with us at all. Then there was a story of his escape from internment in Spanish Morocco in the first year of the war. Nothing disturbed Harry, except now and then the theories and the uncleanliness of 'X'. When sober, he sat in the shadow, propped upon his bed, reading, sipping a glass of tea. Harry threw all the weight of his considerable prestige against the spokesmen of detachment, of the level head. His chosen associates were the roughest diamonds of us all, to whom he was a sort of pandar by conviction. At least once he performed a tenderer office, standing as godfather to the bastard of a departed 'skate' by a Finnish woman. In all of this there must have been a sentimental sort of earthiness. Yet Harry was more than a Chestertonian hearty, a blackleg of the intelligentsia. Travelling home with me, he endured with unruffled composure a ghastly passage round Christmas 1943, though very little, it seemed, awaited him. Returning off leave I was sorry to find no trace in Chatham barracks of his bulky figure, a majestic ruin in matloe's rig.

Shall I go on? – to 'M', melancholy, dyspeptic, stooping, connoisseur of promiscuity, ineffectually penitent about his ageing wife at home? To 'B', living over for the mess in disgusting detail his sexual adventures? To 'R', desperately hen-pecked by his chaste and unattractive girl-friend, scanning his N A A F I ration – 'Where's the Oxo cube?' I could run through the alphabet and still find oddities worth remembering, odd men and the odd things that happened to them. Meanwhile, throughout that summer of 1943, we ran across the road before breakfast to bathe in the Dvina, ducking between the floating logs, and all our hours off watch until the evening we lay upon the sands. The Russians bathed with or without costumes, the bulky women with pick and shovel laboured to repair the road, the merchant-ships still lay in the river, and in the wireless room the long hours on watch ticked by without incident. Now those hours seem sealed in amber, changeless, peaceful, dream images of a sun that never set. Yet equally they were taut and distracted, with questionings, with self-pity, with revulsions. These were private mostly, but they had their public side. Or they seemed to have, to my callow self of those days whose records I now brood upon. 'Unofficial ambassadors' – and what sort of showing did we make? Our educated men? – one crank, one prig, and one drunk. Our culture? – the tasteless bawdry that we shouted at our parties, the maunderings of 'X' about the Apocalypse. Our 'democratic way of life'? – the habits of suburbia, or worse. I have lived to see the Duchy of Luxemburg exclude our football teams because of the barbarous behaviour of their English supporters; and I am compelled to recognize that, had the dice rolled only a little differently, I would have stood in the foreign dock, as depraved as any other fan of Leeds United. And yet for us, somewhere at the centre, there in North Russia in 1943, there burned a delight, an appetite for the abundance of exotic and unlikely experience that clamoured to be known. So we were there not to 'give an example', but to learn. And meanwhile the Russians could see us, accurately enough, as hooligans or cranks, hypocrites or decadents.

However, the Russians probably affixed none of these labels. Natasha, Shura and the rest, who mothered us, made no exception of the rakes and skates. They resented any coarsely insulting behaviour to themselves. But they reserved their contempt for those they called *nyetkulturni*, the exhibitionists, the braggarts, the 'flannel-bo'suns'. One evening in November Granya and I, Pola and Anatoli, went to a movie-film together. Pola and her boy-friend went home by a way more direct, and they began to drink wine. Just as we reached the porch of the long communal house, out rushed Anatoli into the snow, mumbling distractedly, and scrambled across in his stockinged feet, falling down and flinging his arms about. When I went after him and caught him, he made only a token resistance, writhing and crawling on, crying that he would leave her, were it on his hands and knees. Later, sobbing, he was ready to commune with me on the perfidy of the sex. I could tell, from the scorn in Granya's eyes and the shame in Pola's, that it was this sort of posturing, of emotional dishonesty, that was most contemptibly *nyetkulturni* in their eyes. And yet Anatoli, poor fellow, only lacked my resources; my babyish pidgin could be used to touching effect.

The boating parties that set out from a charming little harbour on the way to Salombala, the singing laundresses working at the river's edge further along that way, and Salombala itself, where houses were set far back from streams flowing between, making a prospect almost Dutch though less contrived – these were the scenes of a social history hardly affected, so it seemed, by the last Revolution any more than by others earlier through a long tract of time. The Dynamo stadium itself, though so new, had only brought together into a system dispersed and immemorial habits of association on summer evenings, bibulous courtesies, dances and gossipings.

And of course behind Archangel itself there lay a continent. Drawn back inside the throat of the White Sea, it was a river-port, not really on the coast at all, but quite in the thick of migrations and landward trade-routes, on the gypsy's and the pedlar's circuit, the centre of a region. Murmansk and Polyarno, for all that they lay well up the Kola estuary, had behind them, in time and in space, nothing, or nothing human, only the unimaginable nomadic habits of the Lapp, or sparse brutish fisher-men breaking the ice on as it were Canadian lakes. There hills rose behind the settlements. Here I stood on the outskirts looking out over a feature-less plain, stretching illimitably to small dusty towns in remote and slumbrous provinces, their wooden houses alive with creaks and the drone of flies, scented with comfits and raspberry jam in an old couple's tea; or to the mud, black against thawing snow in churned alley-ways, where Maxim Gorky's savage merchants sweated it out at the ikons, burst in upon the gypsy girls, or leaped from log to log into the turbid river, breaking up a fortune at a whim; or to the mile on mile of swaying grass where the lonely self-maimed beggar, self-styled pilgrim, grimaced and cried to the steppe.

Out of Gorky and Gogol and Chekhov, Leskov and Dostoievsky, these were the images I called up to enhance the images I saw. Did they not so much enhance, as supplant and suppress? Mess-mates told indignant stories of starved babies and victimized women, of a girl who had given fifteen blood-transfusions to get additional bread-coupons. I believed them, and thought guiltily that these comrades of mine had taken greater pains (in the market where British beer-cans, retrieved from scrap-heaps and cut half-down, were sold together with empty jam-jars and odd shoes; in chance encounters about the streets; even in the Interna-tional Club) to get to the heart of Russia. In 1943 the streets of Archangel were still full of *mujiks*. They dogged our heels in gangs, begging for chocolates and cigarettes, impervious to humiliation and our indiffer-ence. When their hopes were dashed they would turn with a vicious mumble of English blasphemy picked up in such encounters before. Just so, cowed and cringing before the *militzia*, they retaliated with derision and abuse when they were out of reach. I see an old crone fumbling down the steps of a street-car while behind her a young and muscular woman beat, her eyes blazing, at the withered arm and the hand still clutching the rail. Once too, we looked out of the windows of Karl Marx House, to see a staggering girl, either imbecile or dead-drunk, beaten and chivvied down the street by a grinning *militzia* man and a ribald crowd, to be flung headlong at last on to the back of a truck.

These, the poker-faced shuffling peasant crowds, were foreign in a way that seemed unbridgeable. I went afterwards to India and looked across the same immeasurable gulf. In India and Russia alike these were people so different from us that we weren't challenged to any human under-standing of them. Granya's mother struck me as very much the same. But with younger Russians like Lyuba and Granya, Serghei and Valentin, or with the unforthcoming Russian sailors, the situation was different. With them, superficially, all the difficulties were small and surmountable. But if so, why did I so often, after spending time in their company, come away feeling that I hadn't made even the most distant contact? And for that matter it certainly wasn't just a matter of distinguishing between the young and the old. For the skivvy of the Wireless Office was quite young, and she, appearing at six in the morning to scrub the office, undoubtedly pretended to be more stupid than she was. Always too deferential, her eyes grew scared and secretive whenever I addressed her. She did not know that she was at war with Italy. And yet an artisan, certainly no younger, knew at once what Italy's capitulation meant – 'You will have bases for bombing the factories in Bohemia.'

If the open market stood for those we could really make no contact with at all, the Dynamo stadium represented all those others with whom we seemed to have more contact than we had. The Russians took their sport seriously. Soviet youth was to be athletic; and so a game of football or volley-ball was momentous, especially when the British were the opponents. Banners blew in the wind, martial music played, the contestants paraded, the crowd watched in dignified and intent silence. The British, sensing and misunderstanding the constraint, reacted against it, making in the midst of the silent throng a vociferous pocket of home-made rosettes, comical bowler-hats, rattles and trumpets. The Russians, with strained smiles or else open disgust, thought us *nyetkulturni*, and in Karl Marx House afterwards the British seethed with stories of discrimination against them by the referees. In a contest the previous summer our football team had gained first place, and in an official report had been placed last 'as not possessing Soviet nationality'. Here at any rate, among the trees of the Dynamo, we encountered the new Russia, Soviet Russia. And all the difficult people one met there, from the frostily reserved to the elaborately formal and the smilingly abusive, were at any rate more accessible than the fawning *mujiks*, with their abject self-effacement. Infrequently, one came across the ardent doctrinaire; and it was beside the tennis-courts of the Dynamo that one of them produced, amid wreathing smiles, all the old gambits, from exploitation of the workers to the lack of a Second Front.

Would it have been in the churches that I might have come closest to the *mujiks*? I should like to think so. And certainly on solitary walks to the quietest corner of quiet Salombala where, among lush grass around the barred church, hundreds of double-barred wooden crosses reared crazily, I felt the truth, reading the epitaphs, of Ivan Bunin's sentiment: 'In this place even a lie was touching.' On the other hand Denis and I stood once, in the metal radiance of ikons, in the other church at Archangel, hearing the incomprehensible Church Slavonic out of the flowing beard of a priest like Moses in what looked like gorgeous brocade: and then, more irrefutably than at any other time in Russia, I felt myself a tourist, irretrievably the outsider. On the October afternoon a woman sobbed throughout the service. And when we came out, there in the churchyard a boy had his boot on the tail of a fat-bellied rat, and lashed it with a whip, while his companions from a few yards away pierced it with their catapults.

In October most of the old hands left for home. Some, like 'Y', were almost in tears with gratitude and delight. Just as many strove desperately to postpone the draft. Just beforehand, the British and the Russian authorities acted in concert, quickly, to prevent a hurried marriage, and another of us was found unconscious, his chest and arms lacerated where he had cut upon them the name of the girl he must leave. There were many demands for the translating and re-translating of love-letters. And half a dozen of us stayed behind to bridge the gap between the departure of the draft for home, and the arrival of their reliefs. When these came, they affronted me. I had forgotten the perky salaciousness of training-camp and barracks. I felt I belonged to an older, more great-hearted generation; and seeing the new hands pursue the same idle girls to satisfy their puny lusts, I thought of their predecessors as deep drinkers, mighty lovers, wild adventurers. This was romantically silly. And yet something, undoubtedly, had happened to those Englishmen between their coming out and their going home. I dare say the new draft, too, changed in the same way.

My own departure was likely within six weeks. And for those last weeks, while winter suddenly clasped the country like a hand, I lived absorbed between Granya on the one hand and my watch-keeping on the other. I was now at last one of the more experienced operators, and was worked hard. For the first time I knew the pleasure of assurance and efficiency in my job, flouting with impunity the prescribed forms, coming on watch late ('Admiralty can wait'), and finding a grim satisfaction in the marvel of communication by wireless, the stir of a flexed finger in London transferring an idea in a moment over a thousand miles, my own impatience disturbing a mind in Brisbane or Vancouver – disturbing it at once, so that 'in touch' meant more than speaking across a continent, meant feeling also. The operator in London drawled with his key, in an exhausted boredom, an extravagant courtesy, so that I smiled wryly. Or, in a burst of passion, he rapped; and I fired too and shot back a rejoinder. Somehow, between the operating-key and the tiny room with Shura's sewing-machine, my life had a crazy completeness. Granya indulged herself in the luxury of our approaching separation, striking a tragic attitude. Meanwhile Henry was implicated in a more than usually riotous brawl, assaulted three Russians, and was arrested. He was sentenced to some weeks in a labour-camp; but that was after I had left.

The end was painful. Did I still want to go home? I no longer knew. Should I be a stranger at home? I was almost sure I should. But home I went, driving on a bitter morning over the frozen river to the ice-breaker at Ekonomia, transferring to a British destroyer, *Otter*, at the Dvina bar. We ran into dirty weather two days out from Vaenga, and then sheered north, for *Scharnhorst* was hunting the outward-bound convoy off North Cape. On Christmas Day, wallowing in huge seas south of Spitzbergen, I heard the end of *Scharnhorst* from the R/T calls of the vessels engaging her. The gale continued, and the convoy rolled on at three to five knots. All fresh water failed, the galley flooded, and a great sea ruined the wardroom flat. At last we left the convoy and ran for the Faeroes. On New Year's Eve of 1943/4, a wild black night, we nosed into Thorshavn.

Somewhere between Ekonomia and Thorshavn the last page slipped over and the book slammed shut. No leavetaking was ever so conclusive, so undeniably the end of a chapter, as my return from Russia. There could never be a going back. And so the experience was complete in itself. It related to nothing before or after. It was a whole chapter to be somehow fitted into my life with no chance of emendation. And at first and for a long time after I returned home, I thought it never could fit. That chapter belonged to a different volume, written in another language. Perspectives there, dimensions and shapes, were crazy by any English standards.

The chapter, already thus complete, contributed even its own epilogue. Denis was a convoy signalman who had come home in October, perhaps the nicest Englishman I knew out there. Chivalrous, and innocently entangled with his Galya, who was a rather brassy piece from Karl Liebknecht Street, he began at once, when home in England, to intrigue to get back. His form of service permitted that. Still, success was unlikely. But in the autumn of '44 I learned that he had worked it, and was off. Later I met him in London. His Galya had sailed for Dickson Island, and been torpedoed. Granya was pleasantly engrossed with one of our more presentable successors. Denis had asked her for a letter for me. Vaguely promising, she procrastinated, and finally let him go without it. She was wise. Thankfully I discontinued the conscientiously ardent letters I had dispatched in her direction since I returned home. But even Denis seemed curiously smaller, almost transparent, as I saw his back dwindle for the last time down the vistas of King's Cross.

5

Plymothians

In 1945, the last year of the war, I married a girl from Plymouth, one of the three home-towns of the Royal Navy. Because I was a wartime sailor, it must seem likely, if we followed the probabilities of fiction rather than fact, that I met my wife on shore-leave, some summer evening on the splendid Hoe; and perhaps that the radiance which at once or gradually enveloped her trim small figure owed something to Charles Kingsley and *Westward Ho!* if not to Thomas Hardy, or at least something to the hanging woods of Mount Edgecumbe and the reaches of the Hamoaze. It wasn't so, however; and if some of these associations have subsequently come to hang about my wife, they are very loose appendages, and have nothing to do with the essence of her, as I know it. However 'literary' I may have been in other responses and relationships, in this, the most intense and consuming relation of them all, I am glad to discern nothing literary in the least.

Of the Plymouth, or more properly the Devonport, which in their physical presence once reached back to Nelson and Collingwood, Boscawen and Drake, I knew, as it happens, nothing whatever. Already when I first made landfall there, months before I met my wife, that

D.D. (left) with shipmates, Ceylon, 1945

Plymouth and that Devonport had been blitzed out of existence; and of that first visit, as of subsequent ones up to D-Day in 1944, I remember indeed very clearly the rude, the desolating anticlimax when, after one lovely prospect after another had glided past us all the way from Start Point or Rame Head, the haven that we finally reached was all squalor and cluttered meanness except where the bombs had scorched out acre on acre of characterless waste. And that, I think I may say, was an accurate prefiguring of how, in less lurid colours, Plymouth was to appear for me through many years after the war when that town, rather than Barnsley, was the 'home' that we escaped to, first from Cambridge and then from Dublin. Nothing more persistently remains with me even now, to characterize Plymouth certainly and perhaps the West Country as a whole, than the obliviousness of most of the inhabitants to the beauties and the history which they live among. It is, to be blunt about it, the most philistine region of England, infinitely more so than the black-ened, ravaged, misshapen industrial midlands where I grew up. So at least it seems to me. It is a judgment that I came to many years ago, and the hygienic sterility which post-war reconstruction has imposed on Plymouth, but on Exeter and Bristol also, surely bears me out. The tourist industry ensures that the innumerable historic and picturesque monu-ments are kept up, cared for, duly exploited. But this caretaking, though

Devonport: the Victualling Yard

for the most part so admirably managed, corresponds to no operation of pious memory in the caretakers. And so it is impossible to say of these churches and manors and whole hamlets, these reaches of coastline and moorland so properly committed to the National Trust, these dolmens and barrows and meetings of the waters, that they are 'cherished'. Preserved, they certainly are – sedulously, and often enough with taste; and one is grateful. But cherished, they are not.

If I seem to speak with undue firmness, my authority is the knowledge that I have of my in-laws. If I call my wife's family 'philistine', I shall seem to be saying that they were raucous, tasteless, aggressive, without principles, vulnerable to the latest whims of commercially incited fashion. They were none of these things. On the contrary they set their faces quite consciously and deliberately against whatever was loud or conspicuous, and against novelty for its own sake. But what they drastically lacked was the faculty of pious memory – except of each other, when dead; and of cherishing – except of each other, while alive. Are these not very great exceptions and concessions to make? Yes, indeed. But this is precisely what I learned from living among them – that one sort of philistinism can not only, with the English, co-exist with unusual human warmth, unusually fierce human loyalties, unusual stability and tenacity, but is actually a pre-condition of such admirable effects. When I first came by this perception – and, as I shall explain in a minute, it was not easily nor soon that I came by it – I related it to 'our finest hour', to the England of 1940 that I had lived through while still too young to take the measure of it. The Churchillian rhetoric of that year has become so flyblown with the passage of time, if indeed it was not tawdry even as Churchill uttered it (though I am of those who think it was not), that it is with defiance I record that for my wife and me, as perhaps for many of our contemporaries, Churchill's speeches of defiance after the evacuation of Dunkirk remained stirring and memorable long after the war was over, and have not lost all capacity to move us, even today. At that point in history, when only the Channel lay between the small, defeated and ill-equipped British forces and the demonstrated might of the German armies, defeat at the hands of the invading Germans was, nonetheless, unimaginable. I knew this for myself, since as a not unimaginative eighteen-year-old patriotically harvesting that summer on the Yorkshire Wolds, I was never required to imagine anything of the sort; how defeat could be, or what defeat might mean. But ten years later, in Plymouth with my kind and generous in-laws, 'unimaginable' had another ring to it. Was not 'imagination' – not of fairyland either, but precisely of history – just what I had now committed myself to, as the cause to which I would (not very heroically, to be sure) dedicate my life? And was I not beginning, reluctantly and uncomfortably, to convict my new kindred of an almost complete blankness in this regard, even as they uncomprehendingly tolerated and even respected my whimsical addiction to it? And if so, how could I not go on to wonder if in one important respect they didn't have right on their side? An imaginative people would *not*, in 1940, have found defeat unimaginable; and imagining it, would they not have been in just that measure susceptible to it? In later years, learning of nations who were more imaginative, of the Irish, the Poles, the Hungarians, who have given to the act of the literary and historical imagination a dignity and centrality that the English have not given it for centuries, learning moreover of the turbulently unstable history of those nations, I was obliged once again to wonder if the English did not owe their comparative stability to the disrespect and tolerant levity with which they might say for instance, to quiet some childhood apprehension of mine, 'That's all in your imagination.' These are disquieting speculations that I have never yet learned how to set at rest; and my mostly unspoken awareness of them has quite often made me a silent traitor in my own chosen camp. That camp, pitifully ill-manned, is devoted to stirring and rekindling imagination in the English. But what if the English do better without it? If they are not, at all events, happier and safer without it? The only step to be taken beyond that is the perilous one of asserting that neither safety nor indeed happiness is a sufficiently lofty goal for a nation to aim at. And in all this the imagination that I have in mind is the one that goes along with cherishing, with pious memory; not at all that quite different messianic imagination that looks forward to 'all things made new', to pie in some post-revolutionary sky. To that imagination I have never been addicted in the least, or never since 1939 when in the sixth form of Barnsley Grammar School I maintained against Donald Chapman, later a Labour M.P. and Peer, the cause of the Finns resisting a Russian invasion.

What may be contended, perhaps indignantly, is that these values and capacities which I gesture at – pious memory, imagination, cherishing – are indeed to be found in the English people; that they are the more deeply rooted for being inarticulate; and that only my own excessive articulacy makes me believe them non-existent when they are not talked about. I know this argument well. It was my own argument through many years early in my marriage, when I came near to idolizing my mother-in-law, very ready to feel ashamed before what I saw as her unreflecting, unargued sturdiness, directness and sanity. I can hardly believe, now that I remember it, how much of virtue I projected on to her, imputed to her – for no better reason than distrust of my own intellectualism. (It is not pretty to remember this, for was it not disloyal to my own parents, who had sacrificed much to give me the intellectualism that I now so readily held cheap? And it is true that in those years I saw my parents rather seldom.) I think than I cannot have revealed to my wife the full intemperate measure of my admiration for her mother. For Doreen, naturally enough, knew her mother better than I did, and must have had sardonic reservations about so much of my enthusiasms as I allowed to show. In particular, as the only bookish child in a family where bookishness was not just unknown but positively and fiercely condemned (Did it not make one 'unsociable'?), Doreen had felt the philistinism of her mother – and of her aunts, for the tribe was profoundly matriarchal – take an aggressive and bludgeoning form, when her schooling was abruptly curtailed precisely because she was so attached to it. (She had escaped – not with a clean break, but through a campaign of attrition sustained over several years – to London, where I met her).

On 10 May 1952, I confided to my journal: 'In my poetry of the last six months I have made concessions to vulgarity – in the shape of point and glitter, striking similes, rhetorical gawds, memorable lines; anything that emphasizes the detail at the expense of the whole. And I shall continue to do so, in hopes of public favour.' And in the pages of the journal which follow begin to appear the poems that I afterwards assembled to make my first collection, *Brides of Reason* (1955). What stands first in that collection is a Plymothian poem, called 'Among Artisans' Houses':

> High above Plymouth, not so high
> But that the roof-tops seem to sweat
> In the damp sea-mist, the damp sea-sky
> Lowers on terraced houses, set
> Like citadels, so blank and high;
> Clothes-lines run to a handy cleat,
> And plots are furiously neat.
>
> There are not many notice this
> Resourcefulness of citizens,
> And few esteem it. But it is
> An outcome of the civic sense,
> Its small and mean utilities;
> A civilization, in its way,
> Its rudiments or its decay.
>
> And if civility is gone,
> As we assume it is, the moulds
> Of commonwealth all broken down,
> Then how explain that this still holds,
> The strong though cramped and cramping tone
> Of mutual respect, that cries
> Out of these small civilities?

It could occur, perhaps, only here,
On these hills over Plymouth Sound,
Where continuity is clear
From Drake to now, where life is bound
Still, though obscurely, to the gear
Traditionally maritime,
And sanctioned by the use of time.

There is no moral to the scene,
Curious relic from the past.
What has and not what might have been
It serves to show now. And at last,
Shortly, nothing will be seen
By which historians may fix
The moral shape of politics.

The house in this poem is the home of Doreen's parents, in Peverell. But it is seen less as the domain of her mother than of her father; a Welsh shipwright in whom I detected, though he was so far from his native ground, a capacity for that pious cherishing of places and customs that I looked for in vain in the family that he, like I, had married into. (I was to write him another Plymothian poem when he died in 1958: 'For an Age of Plastics'.) The question which the poem raises has become for me ever more naggingly unanswerable over the many years since. It nags at me whenever and wherever I am in England, but particularly in the West Country where, since 1976, I have had a little house of my own. It is the question: at what point do the signs of civility, as the poem adumbrates that quality, become so rudimentary or so vestigial that one can no longer defend them, or applaud them, or invest any hope in them?

At any rate, brooding on the meaning for me of the landscape of modern Plymouth, I am inclined to think that what I need to remember from my wartime years is not so much their Russianness, but rather the homelessness – of all of us, English and Scotch, Polish and Russian, German, American. . . . Yet homelessness too falls short of what I want to convey. I think of Graham Greene, that wonderful writer, catching, in *The Third Man*, uncannily and poetically the feel of post-war Europe: 'How quickly one becomes aware of silence even in so silent a city as Vienna with the snow steadily settling.' Ten years at least after that, one experienced – I experienced – that same deathly hush in the half of Budapest called Pest, still after fifteen years barely stirring in the uncleared *débris* made by Russian and German guns. And indeed, later still, in the physically unscathed because neutral city of Zürich, I had the same unnerving sense – that we, those of my generation and older, and whatever our nationality, were phantoms, revenants, the unprovided-for and less than three-dimensional *survivors*. 'Post-war' – the label that made such obvious sense thirty years ago now of course makes no sense to men and women younger than I am. But to me it is meaningful still, and will – I now realize – make all the sense that there ever is for me, at least in the Old World if not in the New. Though no one was killed before my eyes, and although my war was mild indeed compared with what some of my friends experienced, yet I have a fervent sense that whatever years I have lived through since 1945 have been in many ways anticlimactic, on borrowed time. Always the face that rises before my mind's eye, unanswerably enforcing this, is the face of John Bird; school-mate through many years, bird-like according to his name but of a specially plump and liquid sort, as it were a pigeon, his short and already bulky frame crammed implausibly into the R.A.F. uniform in which, after drinking with me and Pip Mitchell in the 'Three Cranes' in Barnsley, he flew to his death not by enemy action but by misjudgment, coming in to land. And how many of those other faces that swim across my memory – Russian and German and Polish and English – did not in fact survive 1945, or did not survive it for long? Much more than Plymouth, that bakelite phoenix of a city rising in surgical sterility from the ashes of its Blitz, Devonport – the one-time much-historied haven that I never knew except in its ruins – has graphed, in the history of its steady strangulation since 1945, the heartlessness, unthinking of course and unintended, with which the wartime survivors have been disregarded, as younger generations have waited for them to die. My wife's uncle, the widower Sidney Weeks – himself no combatant, though in the 1930s a dockyard draughtsman who served in Trincomalee – always for me ranges those foredoomed landscapes, his raking and raincoated stride telling off the miles between Sutton and Stonehouse and St Budeaux, Devonport and Honicknowle.

I have never been in Vienna but once. Or twice rather, coming and going; but in either case only for a three-hour gap between trains – the train from Venice, the train to Warsaw, and the same in reverse, coming back. That was over twenty years ago, August of 1960. And the whole expedition supplied me with experiences – some comical, some frightening, some pathetic – which at long intervals I try to recapture, mostly in verse. But for now it seems right to say that this city which I have never known except by courtesy of Carol Reed and Graham Greene is, as they have re-created it for us, the moral landscape that I have moved in through the last thirty-five years, when I have been most aware of who I was, and what I was doing. There is a wonderful passage when Harry Lime, English in Greene's novel though American when Orson Welles played him in the film, perilously declares himself in a cabin of the great ferris-wheel which, there in the Russian zone of occupation, alone turns still and desolately above the wreckage of the between-the-wars amusement park where smashed tanks have been left to rust in the snow:

> 'In these days, old man, nobody thinks in terms of human beings. Governments don't, so why should we? They talk of the people and the proletariat, and I talk of the mugs. It's the same thing. They have their five-year plans and so have I.'
> 'You used to be a Catholic.'
> 'Oh, I still *believe*, old man. In God and mercy and all that. I'm not hurting anybody's soul by what I do. The dead are happier dead. They don't miss much here, poor devils,' he added with that odd touch of genuine pity, as the car reached the platform and the faces of the doomed-to-be-victims, the tired pleasure-hoping Sunday faces, peered in at them.

It is beautiful there, how Harry Lime's corrupt though genuine compassion enacts itself through the long *drag* of those belated adverbial clauses carrying (how unfeelingly!) their sorry freight of words like 'pleasure-hoping'. The platform, and the faces, and the peering of those faces, are afterthoughts; it is what the syntax of the sentences declares them to be. And I suppose it would not be intolerably fanciful to say that the persistence of the once-imperial capital, Vienna, is itself (since 1945) a sort of afterthought. I have seen such 'pleasure-hoping' on wartime faces in North Russia. Those of us, of many nations, who survived World War Two must, as the years pass, seem more and more like afterthoughts, sometimes in our own self-pitying minds and certainly in the minds of those who come after us. Leonid Brezhnev perhaps is such an afterthought, determined (though wearily, surely) on freezing the western world into the postures that had once made sense, when he was young.

Some English cities – certainly the once great sea-ports like Liverpool or Plymouth, as imperial in their day as Vienna itself – are accordingly haunted places for us, melancholy and moving, so long as we think of them as cities of Europe along with Vienna and Budapest and Zürich. It is thus that such English cities were seen by writers like Greene or Auden who wrote in the 1930s, and that vision is one of the things for which I go back to those authors. Since 1945 the contraction of the once-imperial horizons of the English seems to have meant that for younger people than me, if Plymouth is melancholy at all, its melancholy is merely that of the provinces, something shabbier and fustier, with no historical resonance. Pre-war socialism, though I never embraced it, was genuinely international and had that attraction for me, that it insistently placed England in the context of Europe; whereas post-war British socialism has become more and more a *national* socialism, nourishing insularity and therefore, outside of London, provincialism. And so, when I nowadays walk the streets of Plymouth or Devonport, I feel rather bitterly the loss of a dimension and a resonance that those scenes had for me when I knew them first.

6

Pharisees

No chapter of anyone's life is really closed. No span of years can be sealed off from having consequences. And if any one pretends that some one chapter is so conclusively *over*, he pays the price of it in the ensuing chapter when the consequences, not acknowledged and acted upon, nonetheless work themselves out. So, it seems to me now, did things work out for me, when I returned to Cambridge after the war, determined that my Russian years should be thereafter 'a closed book'. In consequence of that determination, if now I turn my attention from that Russian vista to the time of my life which succeeded it, I see little but blurs and shadows, or else scenes and figures which stand out sharply enough but disconnectedly, casting no shadows at all. I do not mean that it was an unhappy time, for mostly it wasn't. Let's say, soothingly, that it was a time of casting about, making fresh starts, some of them false ones.

The bald record shows none of this. Did I not, when the war was over, return to Cambridge, picking up smoothly enough where I had left off? I picked up indeed, but not smoothly. We all, all of my generation, perhaps in some sort the whole nation, got into harness again. How perverse it must seem, to phrase in this way the switch from war to peace! Was there not on the contrary a feeling of release and relief, of freedoms regained and restored? I suppose there must have been. But in fact, as is tediously well known, the British in those post-war years were exhorted and compelled by Stafford Cripps and the Attlee government to draw in their belts, to 'buckle to'. The metaphors of harnessing seem inescapable. In my case, as I think for many of my Cambridge contemporaries, the harness was 'your career'. Snaffled and bridled, the bit between my teeth, career indeed was what I did, headlong, self-blinkered and at a furious pace, to fetch up, winded and in a lather of sweat, only within the last few years from this present time of writing.

No one compelled me to this. It was what I chose for myself, and everything in my character and my Barnsley conditioning made the choice inevitable. Moreover I suppose that my case must have been representative of us 'scholarship boys' in general. Others among them may have shared with me an additional reason why the harness was welcome; namely, the discovery under wartime conditions of alarmingly unruly proclivities in one's self. For during my sailor's years, in Russia and the Far East and at sea, I had sympathized quite ardently with that 'way of excess' which I saw pursued by some of my mess-mates. I liked the imprudent ones far more than the reliable and responsible. I could see myself going along with a desperado of the lower deck, not indeed as an equal ally but as an admiring and mostly loyal lieutenant. There was that in me which was anarchic and fatalistic; the war had shown it to me, and it frightened me. Already at that time, as over the years since and even in post-war Cambridge when I could afford it, I used for these anarchic potencies the safety-valve of heavy drinking.

But this did not prevent me from being still the youthful prig who had been Douglas's friend. And Douglas of course came back into my life when we each returned to Cambridge in 1946. According to George Eliot, or per-haps to a character in one of her novels, 'A prig is a fellow who is always making you a present of his opinions.' From that mordant indictment I think that both Douglas and I could just about scrape free. But the Oxford Dictionary gives an eighteenth-century sense for 'prig' which I'm afraid fits our case all too neatly: 'A precisian in speech or manners; one who cultivates or affects a propriety of culture, learning, or morals, which offends or bores others; a conceited or didactic person.' And yet if in the late 1940s that was a true bill so far as Douglas and I were concerned, it fitted no less accurately everyone in the university who responded to the presence and the ideology of F. R. Leavis in Downing. To be a member of

East Anglia: Summer

what Leavis promoted as 'a minority culture' one had to be indeed a precisian in speech and, for the most part, in manners also; one had to cultivate propriety of culture which meant necessarily, so the doctrine went, propriety of morals; one had to be a didactic person; and one had to be prepared for others to be affronted, or bored, by one's pretensions. Now, a quarter-century later, I get the impression that the personality thus delineated is still the distinctive product of the Cambridge English School. And nowadays, if the type and its pretensions are among the things that exacerbate me in and about Cambridge, that doesn't mean in the least that I have achieved a position of principled antagonism to that type, or to my own earlier self which conformed to it. On the contrary, though I want to disown that earlier self, I cannot see in good conscience how to do so. I am exhausted by the to-and-fro of my sentiments on this issue, and exasperated at my inability to resolve it. To put it another way, though I sympathize very promptly and warmly with the angry dislike that the prig provokes, I cannot for long trust or respect the heartily permissive common sense that is proposed as an alternative. In politics I can deal with the prig, that is to say, the doctrinaire; I can oppose him and rule him out of court angrily, consistently, and with a good conscience. But this is because I take politics to be in any case a realm of more or less soiled accommodations and approximations, in which the coarse-grained principle of 'live and let live' seems on the whole to do less harm than any other. But in the areas of personal morality and the arts, realms where I expect principles more rigorous and absolute, I cannot see, much as I should like to, how to rule the prig, the precisian, out of court. And indeed this dilemma was, I now recognize, predictable and

Byron's Pool, Grantchester, 1948: long since vanished

inescapable; son of a Baptist deacon and grandson of a Baptist lay-preacher, how could I not have felt some sympathy, however sneaking, with the prig as the eighteenth century defined him? According to the Oxford Dictionary again, 'prig' in the late seventeenth and early eighteenth century was 'applied to a precisian in religion, *especially a nonconformist minister*' (italics mine). The Dissenters' conception of 'a gathered church', gathered *from* the world and in tension with it, cannot help but be the model for Leavis's minority culture. But it was some years later that I worked this out for myself, and documented it in a handful of poems. And although what guided me were the writings of a Cambridge historian of the dissenting churches, Bernard Manning of Jesus, the reading was done in Dublin, where the disestablished Church of Ireland satisfied the need, bred in me as a child, to envisage my church as in tension with the state, by no means coterminous with it as the Church of England must pretend to be. Years later again, after I had myself bandied about the expression 'the Establishment', in its cant sense as referring to what sustains an inert consensus in intellectual and artistic life, I realized that properly speaking there is only one Establishment in English life, and that is the Established Church.

Portugal Place, Cambridge

At any rate, between 1946 and 1950 my sympathy with the prig was not sneaking at all, but fervent and militant. Those were the years when *Scrutiny* was my bible, and F. R. Leavis my prophet. It is hard for me now to be fair to myself of those years. Perhaps the best that can be said for him is that, for good and pressing reasons, he was no longer the young man of 1940 who could dream of reading, in time, along every shelf in the English Faculty Library. Subsisting on a student's grant in four draughty and mouse-infested rooms over the village store in Trumpington, my wife and I could not fail to see that I had to become a breadwinner as quickly

Cambridge: King's Parade from Trinity Street

and efficiently as possible; and since, thanks to taking good classes in the Tripos, it seemed that my livelihood was to be that of a university teacher, the sheer bulk and expanse of accredited literature even in our native language was no longer, as it had been in Marlowe Road, an endless series of enticing vistas, but on the contrary presented itself as a daunting and unmanageable field through which I must somehow cut a few narrow swathes. And for this, *Scrutiny* was irreplaceable. Every issue of the magazine made me a present of perhaps a dozen authors or books or whole periods and genres of literature which I not only *need* not read, but *should not*. To be spared so much of literature, and at the same time earn moral credit by the exemption – no wonder that I loved *Scrutiny*, and Leavis's *Revaluation*, and his *New Bearings in English Verse*! Of course it was not what Leavis and his collaborators had in mind, nor did I have it consciously in mind myself. But looking back, I can have no doubt that this was one great attraction for me, perhaps the greatest, in the sort of criticism associated with Leavis's name. And indeed at some stage of his education every student needs, and even deserves, to be presented with a rigorously narrow canon of approved reading such as Leavis, not alto-gether fairly, was widely held to be providing. An immersion in *Scrutiny*, even an infatuation with it, is no bad thing if only one can be sure that the student will in due course pull out of it, or pass beyond it. But of course there is no way of ensuring this; and there's the danger.

There are other dangers. It is by thinking myself back into the person I was then, that I can enter imaginatively into the thoughts and feelings of the fanatic, for instance the committed revolutionary, the persecutor, the gauleiter, the commissar. Perhaps I should be grateful. Certainly, with-out having undergone this relatively innocuous experience of fanatical commitment, I should have no experiences of my own to call upon, to understand in imagination the appeal for a Nazi or a Communist of the image of a band of embattled brothers, or the psychological security of having, for the assessing of each new experience, a body of scriptural texts to refer to. I could elaborate: for instance, ruthlessness as a virtue, blind obedience as another. . . . But I do not want to be, or to seem, unfair and disproportionate. Simply I put it on record that, however it may have been with others, introspection after the fact assures me that my *Scrutiny* allegiance was fed from sources as deep and as dubious as these.

At this time when I most venerated Leavis – always from a distance, for I was not of his college, and only once was I ever in his house – there stood behind him, so far as I was concerned, a figure of even greater authority, T. S. Eliot. This was to change, and indeed in those very years it was changing, as Leavis, more and more fully convinced of the moral genius of D. H. Lawrence, uncovered evidence of how consistently Eliot had blocked the rating of Lawrence's writings at what Leavis took to be their true worth. To champion Lawrence, Leavis was to have increasingly harsh things to say about what he saw as the humanly constricted nature of Eliot's Anglo-American achievement. But in the 1940s Leavis's second thoughts about Eliot were only just beginning to show themselves; and our respect for Leavis rested in part, and quite properly, on his claim to have been one academic critic of literature who showed himself abreast of the most distinguished creative breakthrough of his time, Eliot's *The Waste Land*. For me, and those of my friends who like me were committed to poetry rather than other forms of literature, it was the young Leavis's championing of the poet Eliot that still carried weight. Eliot, as critic even more than as poet, dominated our horizon. It is hard to convey the virtually unchallenged eminence that Eliot continued to enjoy, in literary circles in Cambridge as elsewhere, through the 1940s and well into the 1950s. Those who did not experience it are right to be sceptical, for it is surely very rare for a poet, still writing and publishing as Eliot was, to enjoy the sort of pre-eminence that he had. Nevertheless it was indeed so; and the first of my all too many manifestoes about poetry, printed in those years mostly in Cambridge magazines, characteristically gen-uflected towards the author of *The Waste Land* and *Four Quartets*, and staked out whatever position they timidly sought to maintain, by veering a very few points away from something that Eliot had said in print.

When all is said and done (I tell myself now, indignantly), I already had something in common with Boris Pasternak and Alexander Solzhenitsyn. At no cost to myself I shared with them the smell of black bread, the look of a Russian provincial street in wartime, the wild figures and faces that loomed up on those streets out of an unimaginable hinterland in space and time. Illusion? It is *not* an illusion. And how, with that experience behind me, can I ever have joined with academic fervour in English arguments for or against F. R. Leavis, in American altercations for or against Yvor Winters? Let me not luxuriate in self-reproaches. Those were after all, I now remember, the years when I tried without success to make my shore-leave sailor's Russian into something more reliable. Those were the years when, stamping irritably hard on the bicycle pedals, I surged home along Trumpington Road with, in the basket hitched to my handlebars, battered books picked up from David's bookstall – Babel and Valentin Ivanov, Bunin and Sholokhov, in wretched translations. In those years even, I first tried to grapple with Pasternak, retiring baffled and angry. I knew there was something there, in those authors, which would, if I could only get hold of it, hitch up into my life past experiences that otherwise I could find no room for. And even now I can't easily define the extra dimension that my Russian enthusiasms have given me. But I think of Konstantin Paustovsky, in *The Story of a Life*, when he tells of ferrying the wounded through Moscow in the First World War:

> Ah, those Lefertovo nights! Nights of war, of suffering, and of wondering about man's road through this tortuous, hard life. These were the nights when I really grew up. With every day, worthless parts of my earlier conception of reality shriveled up and blew away. I began to see life as something hard and demanding, requiring constant work to clean it of its dirt, pus and deceit, and I began to see its magnificence and its simplicity.

There is more than a touch here of a peculiarly Russian sort of boringness and dishonesty. But that is only the rhetorical surplus or spin-off from what is irreplaceably shaming to us in the Russian writers of our day, not least Paustovsky himself: the generosity of their feeling, their determination to call down benedictions on the life which, on any balance-sheet of assessable profit and loss, has treated them so much more scurvily than it has treated us. Nowhere for me does that generosity count for so much as in the accounts that they give of love between the sexes, the unembarrassed fulness with which a Pasternak or a Solzhenitsyn treats of relations between man and woman as responsible and dignified persons, relations joyously comprehending desire yet not hypnotized by it. I look in vain for any comparable image of that, in my British or American contemporaries and forerunners, including those whom Leavis and Winters most applauded.

And yet that too is ultimately beside the point. What my Russian time should have taught me, what it *did* teach me – though I forgot the lesson, and I forget it still, much of the time – is that the writer's sole duty is to report what was, *as it was*; and that, in the interest of serving that overriding obligation, he must be prepared to be numbered among the criminals, the perverts, the barbarians, even the unfeeling administrators. In his other capacities – and he should have them, for no creature is much more piteous than the writer who is writer and nothing else, writer all through – he is required, like any other citizen, to take sides; and to take his side not idly and inconsiderately, but with scruple and imagination. But while he is a writer, and insofar as he is a writer, he cannot afford to take sides, but must stand above or apart from them all – not dispassionately indeed, but on the contrary with a quite feverish passion. That passion is not a compulsion, as for their different discreditable reasons the critics and the general public want it to be. If the writer's passion were compulsive then he could not be held to account for any of his actions, whereas for the mere dignity of his calling he has to be, and will demand to be, held accountable. It is an American not a British idiom that conveys my sense of this: for the writer, insofar as he *is* a writer, he 'lays it on the line'. He relates things as he has found them to be, in the world and in himself; and he may be as aghast as any of his readers at what he finds himself saying, at what (in despite of his own most cherished wishes) he finds himself required, by the mere facts of the case, to record. That is what I learned, not just from the Russian writers I read in translation, but from trying to take stock of my own Russian experiences even as I experienced them. It is a simple lesson that I have never learned well enough.

And is it so simple after all? For Dostoievsky mattered greatly to Douglas Brown, as Tolstoy mattered to F. R. Leavis. And the Russian literary tradition, more than any other in Europe, has a dimension that the Russians call 'civic', which we may call, approvingly or not, 'moralistic'. That is to say, the Russians have asked of their writers that they be, not merely witnesses, but 'teachers'. I have been content for the most part to know about this dimension, rather than know it. Belinsky, Dobrolyubov, Chernyshevsky – these were Russian critics of the nineteenth century who hectored the Russian writers of their day on their duties to their public. And when I was writing my doctoral dissertation on an Anglo-Russian theme in the vain hope of achieving command of Russian, I had to take note of these men. But I passed over them as fast as I dared, because of a not unreasonable prejudice which saw them as the baleful forerunners of the Zhdanovs of those post-war years, who were then hectoring Russian writers still more brutally, and silencing some like Zoshchenko and Akhmatova who would not fall in with their directives. Later, when I began to read Vladimir Nabokov, I delighted in the lofty derision which, in a book like *The Gift*, he heaped on the Belinskys and Chernyshevskys. Yet even so I knew that Nabokov couldn't be right, when he made of Pushkin only an idle voluptuary with a rhyming itch. Pushkin, I saw, was a conscience as well as a consciousness. And from Baptist pulpits that I once had sat under, had I not heard 'witness' used in a way that did not exclude 'teacher' nor even 'prophet'? Thus there was after all, though at that time I was loth to admit it, a connection between my Russian enthusiasms and my being 'a Leavisite'.

The connection, I see, is in fact quite laughably evident in a poem that I worked at in those years. 'Pushkin. A Didactic Poem' (I writhe somewhat at the youthful aplomb of the title) appears in my *Collected Poems* in a version drastically abbreviated from the sheaf on sheaf of pages that I pored over and shuffled around through many weeks and months in Trumpington. It is extremely prosaic, and was meant to be; for already then I had conceived, from my reading of *Four Quartets*, an enterprise which I suppose I have never since given up – the incorporating into verse of more and more of the prose virtues, so as to see how near to prose

81

poetry can come while still remaining poetry. But in that pursuit it matters greatly what *sort* of prose your poetry is borrowing from and alluding to. And in my 'Pushkin', it is clear to me now that the prose in question is the prose of *Scrutiny* – not Leavis's own prose, which is distinctive, but the sort of prose, at all events of vocabulary, which Douglas and I expected from the undergraduates we had begun to supervise. (And indeed Douglas I remember helped me with the poem, or tried to – chiefly by casting a worried eye at each of the lyrical quatrains which, as I hoped, allayed the didacticism.) When the poem was more or less 'finished', there was no question what magazine I should submit it to. *Scrutiny*, of course! Silence fell. Not from Leavis himself, whom I would not have dared to approach, but from one of his co-editors, H. A. Mason, I ascertained that the packet had in fact been delivered. Then silence fell again. This went on for eighteen months, to the point where I avoided Mason's eye as much as he avoided mine, in the catalogue room of the University Library. In the end I desperately asked if the thing could at all events be returned to me. And so it was, with never a yea or a nay, no word of comment, not even a covering letter. I do not blame Mason, for it was far from clear that those whose names appeared with Leavis's on the masthead of *Scrutiny* had any real share of editorial authority. But at any rate I know at first hand how uninterested *Scrutiny* was in poems that were sent in, how much at a loss to know how to deal with them. I resented the discourtesy, and Douglas was discomfited by it. I resent it still, and if I am now less than fair to Leavis and to *Scrutiny*, I have my reasons.

But it is a hopeless business after all, trying to be fair to Leavis. He was never fair himself. Was Lawrence 'fair' to Galsworthy or Middleton Murry? Was William Blake 'fair' to Joshua Reynolds? Is Solzhenitsyn 'fair'? (One gathers not.) These are writers – and by the end Leavis was taking Blake's part along with Lawrence's – who cannot stop for fair-mindedness, judiciousness, holding the balance steady. In this they are Romantics, or at least they profit by and count on the Romantic conviction that a sufficient head of passion in a man absolves him from practising the cooler virtues. And those of us who still try for such coolness find, as soon as we would take account of these people, not that our fair-mindedness fails us, but that it shoots past the mark or falls short of it, is deflected at a tangent, is beside the point. Not only is it not the standard that they ask to be judged by, it is a standard that yields no illumination, but hands down a judgment that is either shrill or fawning. The most one can do is to try again and again, never conclusively; and here I am trying once more . . .

It is a Russian voice, Joseph Brodsky's, which now, even as I write, declares with a cold fury:

There is something in the consciousness of literati that cannot stand the notion of someone's moral authority. They resign themselves to the existence of a First Party Secretary, or of a Führer, as to a necessary evil, but they would eagerly question a prophet. This is so, presumably, because being told that you are a slave is less disheartening news than being told that morally you are a zero. After all, a fallen dog shouldn't be kicked. However, a prophet kicks the fallen dog not to finish it off but to get it back on its feet. The resistance to those kicks, the questioning of a writer's assertions and charges, comes not from the desire for truth but from the intellectual smugness of slavery. All the worse, then, for the literati when the authority is not only moral but also cultural.

The *literati* whom Brodsky lashes are those in the Soviet Union who were outraged when Nadezhda Mandelstam, in her *Hope Against Hope*, indicted for the persecution and death of her poet–husband not just the Soviet state but Soviet society as a whole, including, quite notably indeed, its literary intelligentsia. But by the plainest implication Brodsky indicts also the American *literati* who read him in *The New York Review of Books*. Just so did Leavis indict the English *literati* for their treatment of Lawrence among others. Just so did Douglas indict the Cambridge *literati* who attacked and derided Leavis. And the kicks which they directed at those sad dogs, England and literary Cambridge, were meant to get the poor brutes back on their feet. Their motives in short were patriotic.

What for me obscured these parallels, and in some measure obscures them still, is the manifest difference of scale. The British *literatus* is not enslaved so patently as the Russian is; Lawrence did not suffer as Mandelstam did; Mrs Mandelstam was victimized as Leavis wasn't; and Brodsky speaks as an exiled inhabitant of two cultures, in a way no British expatriate can. This difference of scale is important, and is habitually overlooked by those who nowadays speak up for Leavis, if only because they tend to be – as their master was, before the end – defiantly or unthinkingly insular. (Is it too much to hope that we have seen the last of letters to the press about whether Leavis and his wife were or were not passed over for promotion in Cambridge, and if so whether excusably? For heaven's sake, what we are talking about is *suffering*!) All the same, in all these cases the principle at issue is the same; and Brodsky names it – 'someone's moral authority'. Mrs Mandelstam, he says, possessed this authority. He does not say – he explicitly denies – that she earned it by her sufferings. Indeed, while on the one hand it is not something that some people are born with, on the other hand for Brodsky this authority is not *earned* at all, in any ordinary sense of earning. It was something that Nadezhda Mandelstam came by; and Brodsky is quite certain how she came by it – by memorizing, in an unusually literal and urgent sense, a range of Russian texts beginning

83

with, and centred upon, her husband's poems and Akhmatova's. This is what he means by saying that her authority was 'moral but also cultural'; indeed, if I understand him, it could be the first only because it was the second. What her memoirs give us, Brodsky says, or at least what they give to Russians, is 'the view of history in the light of conscience and culture'; and her authority resides in the capacity to take that view. As much I think can be said, and ought to be said, of Leavis.

Neither of them, neither the Russian woman nor the Englishman, *got things right*. Brodsky makes no bones about Nadezhda's lack of humility. And he concedes with perfect equanimity that she was 'terribly opinionated, categorical, cranky, disagreeable, idiosyncratic'; and that 'many of her ideas were half-baked or developed on the basis of hearsay'. Every one of these charges can be brought with justice against Leavis. Nor is anyone pretending that these things don't matter. But with Brodsky's help we begin to apprehend a sort of authority which on the one hand is more than mere overbearing force of personality, which on the other hand has little to do with racking up high scores on the scales of the true and the good. Rather, it seems, the authority is known by the *view* which it is able to take, a view of *history*, a view remarkable for rangingness ('culture') and for earnestness ('conscience'). It is in this way that I, who in Douglas knew such an authority at first hand, can recognize in him and in Leavis a sort of greatness which is not diminished by the mistakes they made, nor by their arrogance, nor by the bad intellectual habits they had, nor by the effects they brought about, dubious and at times downright bad, in the people they influenced, including me. In what respect, then, were they great? One possible answer, which will embarrass many, is that they were great as patriots.

7

Dubliners

After the war, when I was a research student in Cambridge, there came to my college the Anglo-Irishman Peter Allt, then collaborating with G. D. Allspach in America on the variorum edition of the poems of Yeats. I was crankily suspicious of all sorts of things in those days, and a certain largeness of manner in Allt, his affecting a silver-knobbed cane, and his elaborately allusive conversation, damned him in my eyes as affected. Later, when I had the chance of a post in his old university, Dublin, he exerted himself to advise me and write on my behalf. When I secured the post and left Cambridge, I took with me Allt's advice to get to know his friend, Joe Hone, the biographer of Yeats and George Moore, of Swift and Berkeley and Tonks.

I had never before met a worthy from a previous generation, and I was shy, uncertain how to conduct myself. So I let a long time elapse before I called on Joseph Hone; and after that, still diffident, I did not pursue the acquaintance. This was a pity. For Hone, as Allt had hinted, was a lonely man; how lonely, I could not conceive until I had entered more fully into the life of Ireland, particularly of that Ireland which lay behind the shabby grandeur of Trinity College. There was, for instance, much later in my Trinity years – perhaps one Trinity Monday when Hone gave a memorial oration on Berkeley – an occasion when he carried me off (though that expression is quite out of keeping with Hone's melancholy and deafness) to take tea in the Kildare Street Club. The club itself, dingy and massive at the bottom of Kildare Street, with its notoriously malicious native carvings of billiard-playing monkeys, was a symbol already platitudinous of the vanished Ireland of the Ascendancy landlords. It was known to me only as a spiteful joke, a forty-year-old anomalous survival; but to Hone, apparently, its dusty glooms were still a natural haunt. This pathos in the occasion is pointed up for me when I recall that another at the tea party was Mrs Starkie, mother of Walter Starkie, the Hispanist and ex-fellow of Trinity (whom I had met), and of Enid Starkie, famous around Oxford as the king-maker for the Chair of Poetry. I do not remember if it was then or later that I knew Mrs Starkie through the pages of her daughter's autobiography, *Lady's Child*, a little-known book which evokes the Dublin of James Joyce as seen from a level of society that Joyce could not aspire to; the unbelievably solid-seeming, stately and sumptuous world of the Edwardian viceroys. Through that book, where there is I think passing mention of 'the Hone boys', Mrs Starkie herself moves, a society hostess, young and beautiful, reigning remotely over a household of servant hierarchies. One could not help but see how for her, as in some measure for Hone also, the passage of decades could only augment their bewilderment that a world so substantial should have vanished so utterly. And yet Hone in other ways lived much more in the present than anyone around him, reading for instance, and wanting to discuss, *The Human Age* of Wyndham Lewis, a late work that had just come out. This must have made for loneliness from another direction. And if Ireland could not be blamed for his past that had vanished, it might justly be held to account for the present that Hone acknowledged as Ireland for the most part would not.

In those last years his interests were more philosophical than literary. In fact I suppose his interest in literature had always been the biographer's. And this meant that the only keen interest we had in common was Berkeley. Yeats had written the Introduction to Hone's and Rossi's life of the philosopher, and Hone had edited and printed in Dublin Berkeley's pamphlet on Irish economics, 'The Querist'. As for me, I had already discovered in Berkeley the only philosopher I am able to read with pleasure and at least the illusion of understanding.

Among the rather few men in Trinity who had a more than Irish reputation, there was A. A. Luce, a Senior Fellow who, as I discovered gradually and with astonishment, had forced through almost single-handed a radically new understanding of Berkeley's philosophical position. Bald as an egg, the domed head bent from the spare body with pontifical courtesy, his hard blue eyes would wrinkle and the long lips wreathe in a smile too engaging to be wholly frank, as he pretended not to

My father and my son: County Dublin, 1955

understand my approach to Berkeley through style, through vocabulary and polemical method. My interest in this, and Luce's unexpected though unconvinced indulgence towards my speculations, made me like him and relish his personality. In this I stood apart from my friends and contemporaries on the Trinity faculty, who saw him as a man of one idea (or rather of two, for angling was his other absorbing interest), and above all as a formidable college politician pledged to, as they thought, reactionary policies, and in particular to keeping for the Senior Fellows a monopoly of administrative power. Soon after I went to Trinity in 1950, the death of Provost Alton precipitated a palace revolution which dislodged Luce and the Senior Fellows from their pre-eminence; but of this I knew little, and sought to know no more, for power-politics, at least in a sphere so restricted, held no interest for me. (Years later, when I was at the University of Essex with Albert Sloman, an ex-T.C.D. Englishman like myself, my uncomprehending impatience with such concerns was to cost me dear.) Certainly I was disappointed in the Senior Fellows generally (though W. R. Fearon was an exception) that they murmured 'inaccuracy' when there was talk of an honorary degree for Hone from what was, after all, his spiritual or cultural home; and I thought I detected a lack of cordiality in Doctor Luce when I brought Joseph Hone to dine in college.

Luce after all, though English by origin, was Hone's contemporary. Tom Johnston, my rector in Raheny, remembered him as Captain the Reverend Arthur Luce of the Trinity College Training Corps, pledged in 1916 to protect the college against those rebels and gunmen who now, forty years later, were at the head of affairs in the Republic. And for that matter I knew in his last years another Senior Fellow, an Englishman of a yet earlier generation, the legendary figure Sir Robert Tate, university orator, eccentric, writer of Latin verses, who was said to have earned his

Ireland's Eye: from the Hill of Howth

knighthood by commanding – though *in absentia* – the college's cadets against the insurrection.

However, that evening when Hone was my guest, we found sufficiently appropriate company. For my professor, H. O. White, had brought as his guest the poet Austin Clarke, younger than Hone certainly, yet with interests that should have coincided with his. Perhaps they did, and perhaps Hone enjoyed himself. It was difficult to tell; for his unpopularity was easier to understand after an hour of his crushed and defeated manner, and his exaggerated sense of his own decrepitude. The only image I retain from the evening is of Hone cupping his ear to have a comment by Clarke repeated to him, and then, having got the gist of it, remarking conclusively, '*I* never found Yeats a poseur.'It showed unwonted spirit, and abides with me as the most gallantly unpersuasive of white lies.

It is likely enough, in any case, that Clarke was 'taking a rise' out of the company he was in. For in the corroding malice of his conversation there was always a special place for Yeats; and it would be in character for Clarke to pluck that string all the more, in the presence of such devoted Yeatsians as Hone and 'Ho' White. It was said – and certainly the printed evidence supported it – that the elderly Yeats, having two younger Irish poets on whom to bestow his blessing, all too pointedly passed over Clarke in favour of Fred Higgins. What is not in question is that Clarke was an incomparably better poet than Higgins, and indeed much the best poet to have flourished in Ireland since Yeats first appeared. Not that Clarke could be said to have flourished. His career and Hone's could complement each other, and fit together so as to image between them the life of the mind in republican Ireland. Born a Dublin Catholic not at all of the gentry class, Clarke had years before fallen foul of clerical orthodoxy over marital matters. For this reason or some other he was, of the many Irish Catholics who are anticlerical in private, the only one in my time who was anticlerical consistently, almost obsessively, in the public prints. His touch was admirably feline, never indignant. The *faux-naïf* mockery is at its most entertaining in 'A Penny in the Clouds', his account of how he visited the famous pilgrims' mountain, Croaghpatrick; though not much less good is a further chapter of memoirs which he first printed in *Irish Writing*, where he pretends that the broad black hat he adopted in youth and had worn ever since as properly poetical habit, being confounded with the garb of a priest, brought him all kinds of special attention and unwanted solicitude. Or again there is, with the added gravity of verse, 'St Christopher':

> Child that his strength upbore,
> Knotted as tree-trunks i' the spate,

Became a giant, whose weight
Unearthed the river from shore
Till saint's bones were a-crack.
Fabulist, can an ill state
Like ours, carry so great
A Church upon its back?

Acrid short poems like this, verse of such muscularity, such imaginative wit ('Unearthed the river from shore'), Clarke published, if that is the word, in flimsy pamphlets printed apparently in his own backyard. The same self-wounding perversity crowded these, almost the only poems from Ireland that were not blighted by provincialism of technique, with references so local and topical, so compact and cryptic, as to be unfathomable except by Irishmen of a particular cast of mind and a particular generation.

And this was only the beginning of his perversity. The writer of verse like this, which demanded for its appreciation precisely the attention recommended by modern criticism, in his own weekly reviewing for *The Irish Times* mocked with malice every pretension of the vanguard, and appeared to align himself with the most reactionary taste. In fact it was only an appearance: for Clarke's cynicism was complete, and his irony would undercut every position, conservative no less than 'progressive'. He was never so happy as when he cut the ground from under his own feet. He did so, in theocratic Ireland, whenever he indulged his anticlericalism, just as, whenever he gibed at Yeats, he undermined whatever chance he had with the Anglo-Irish. His spiteful reviewing closed to him the small society that might yet have remained open, the society of the few and demoralized, unaffiliated intellectuals. When I first went to Dublin, Clarke's name was anathema, for instance, to Patrick Kavanagh and Valentine Iremonger, and other writers for two magazines soon afterwards dead, *The Bell* and *Envoy*. Reading his reviews I could see why, and excusably supposed that his own verse could not be worth reading. It was only later, having read it, that I realized how characteristic it was for Clarke to have manoeuvred so that he had all the penalties of the official poet with none of the privileges, beyond a precarious weekly income from his *Irish Times* reviewing and a regular programme with Radio Eireann. Uncrowned laureate of a country where his own books were banned, Clarke, one can only suppose, took a twisted satisfaction from the incongruity, and did his best to heighten it.

It wasn't clear whether the same self-spite had contrived it so that Clarke was unknown to those foreign publics by which other Irish authors managed to make a living. Certainly it wasn't that Clarke, out of timidity or pride, had never established foreign bridgeheads. He had known Bloomsbury in the twenties, and still sometimes availed himself of chances of reviewing in England, though for preference (perversely again) in anonymity and at a 'middlebrow' level. And his *Collected Poems*, of which years of hunting in bookshops have never brought me a single copy, had been brought out in England before the war. On the other hand Clarke, for all his mocking and caustic eye, was still in literary matters a nationalist. His subjects, until he turned to the late satirical epigrams, were all taken from Ireland of the legendary and heroic, or else of the medieval, periods. And his technical innovations, some of great interest to me, came of the importing into English verse of modified interlacements of rhyme and assonance, from old poetry in Irish. It would (I saw) be a characteristic quirk for Clarke to interpret his nationalism as requiring him to frustrate any non-Irish reader.

The broad black hat and long black coat were not unnecessary. For underneath the hat the small narrow face, with its lean reddish jowls, was undistinguished. There was a certain slow mobility of feature – his speech also was slow – and a distinctively crooked, tight-lipped smile. But at receptions and parties – to which, surprisingly, he was not averse – it was not a face to catch or invite attention. I think Clarke's only confidant among younger men was Sean White, the editor of *Irish Writing*, in whom I thought I detected, though at an early stage, the same self-destructive nihilism. Once at least I went with White to visit Clarke in Templeogue, hard by that house whence in the 1840s Charles Lever rode each day to his editor's chair with the *Dublin University Magazine*, daring the hostility of the Repealers. I remember too driving him into the city from a party in Palmerston Park, through evening sunlight athwart the splendid cliff-like curve of Harcourt Street, expostulating with him about his reviewing. There was also a moment in the dark outside the students' little theatre in Trinity when, thrilled by the performance, just over, of Yeats's 'Purgatory', I had to hear him seriously jeering, 'Rhetoric!' There were other encounters. But before I left Dublin the last, surely, was in a pub on Leeson Street, after a triumphant reading in University College by Robert Frost; there W. R. Rodgers, silkily solemn and low-voiced, talked scandal to Clarke about Joyce's milking of his benefactors, and so allayed for both of them the soreness of having been outmatched by the illustrious American's practised manipulation of his audience.

There was something very Irish about that. But I was reluctant to draw, from the case of Clarke, the facile and predictable conclusion that the Irish were 'impossible'. No doubt they were. But the tortuous logic behind Clarke's attitudes was only an extreme and therefore instructive example of how impossible it was for the writer, British or American no less than Irish, to find a right and plausible position vis-à-vis his public, achieved or potential. If Frost's performance represented one solution, Clarke's cattiness was another, in all its tormentedness perhaps more honest.

Sometime during our Dublin years I was made aware – I think by Owen Sheehy Skeffington – of a prodigy called Brendan Behan. As I recall, Behan was described to me in just those terms – as 'prodigy', a house-painter, drunken moreover, who turned out miraculously to be a good, not to say a great, writer. I would not have any of that. For such prodigies, such miracles, I had in any case more scepticism than was proper. Only since then, and slowly, have I brought myself to acknowledge the authentic miracle of John Clare. And yet, did I not have much excuse? On the one hand all the serious writers of my generation had had to fight their way into print, in the teeth of an irrationalist theory of poetry which had seemed to be safely scotched until re-illumined potently by that Welsh miracle, half-prodigy half-charlatan, the doomed and disgusting, self-diagnosing and at last self-denouncing Dylan Thomas. In Behan as Dublin gossip reported him to me I detected, at best, a phenomenon of the same kind; *at best*, I say, for neither then nor since have I detected in the Irish self-destroying prodigy that astonishing verbal inventiveness which the Welsh prodigy – 'the Rimbaud of Cwmdonkin Drive', to adopt his own lethally accurate self-description – so prodigally exploited and per-verted. What I did not sufficiently allow for is the pressure exerted by the dominant British culture, English, so as to distort exponents of the other British cultures – Welsh and Irish and Scottish – into becoming just what Thomas and Behan became: licensed buffoons and zanies, stage-Welsh-men and stage-Irishmen, rewarded by the English for exposing all over again the picturesque incapacity of the Brython or the Gael when released from England's apron-strings. I wasn't unaware of this, but I didn't let it count with me, compassionately. Why should I have? Did not I, an English writer, see my own English writings year after year overlooked by the English public in favour of these picturesque and spectacular Welsh or Irish products, which grabbed the headlines and the audiences? I remem-ber the bitter resentment I felt, perhaps in 1959 or 1960, at seeing Behan's *The Hostage* billed among superlatives outside a London theatre. And it is no comfort to me now, to learn that Behan himself felt betrayed or selfbetrayed by *The Hostage* because of the drastic changes he had drunk-enly allowed Joan Littlewood to make in his script. Besides, I had met once or twice, and was constantly made aware of, another of the same ilk though not quite so self-destructive: Patrick Kavanagh, author of *The Great Hunger*, ploughboy from County Monaghan. Kavanagh, I perceive, still counts for a good deal with my friends among Irish writers, such as Seamus Heaney. And I can understand why. Yet Kavanagh, though his poems were for the most part genuinely conceived, was consistently slipshod in his execution. Only today, in 1979, I see described as 'brilliant' his poem, 'Memory of Brother Michael':

> It would never be morning, always evening,
> Golden sunset, golden age –
> When Shakespeare, Marlowe and Jonson were writing
> The future of England page by page,
> A nettle-wild grave was Ireland's stage.
>
> It would never be spring, always autumn
> After a harvest always lost,
> When Drake was winning seas for England
> We sailed in puddles of the past
> Chasing the ghost of Brendan's mast.
>
> Culture is always something that was,
> Something pedants can measure,
> Skull of bard, thigh of chief,
> Depth of dried-up river.
> Shall we be thus for ever?
> Shall we be thus for ever?

When Kavanagh was told that the lifetime of Shakespeare and Jonson saw in Ireland a last glorious efflorescence of lyric poetry in Gaelic, he shrugged and said that his verses were 'good poetry but bad history'. Surely he was wrong; his lines are genuine, but they are not *good*. Metrically, for instance, they are all over the place; and it's astonishing that Heaney, who in these matters exacts so much of himself, should of his predecessors (so long as they are Irish) be content to exact so little. I at any rate, trying in my Dublin years to school myself so as to practise verse as a *strict* discipline, could not afford to be indulgent towards a Behan or a Kavanagh. Be they Irish or be they English (and their English associates were mostly worse), they were for me bad news and bad medicine.

I was not told at that time of Brendan Behan's long association with the I.R.A., nor of his poems and other writings in Irish. To me, as an Englishman, not all could be divulged – least of all by Owen Skeffington who, though a socialist, and protestant, and thoroughly anglicized by his protestant education, was the son of one of the most authentic martyrs to British violence at the time of the Black-and-Tans; who therefore doubt-less harboured, though at a level far below his consciously 'progressive' agnosticism, anti-British sentiments of perhaps peculiar virulence. (I remember that we disagreed explicitly only once – about the treatment of William Joyce, 'Lord Haw-Haw'.) Yet, though I never met Behan, and as it turns out never knew more than half of his story, it still seems to me I was right to give to Austin Clarke the respect that I withheld from Behan and Patrick Kavanagh.

What I have always liked about the Irish Republic, and what I like still when I go there as I try to do once a year, is that it is, of all the societies that I know, the least 'sexy'. This reason for liking it, and indeed approving it, runs so directly counter to what is the accepted wisdom, among the halfway sophisticated Irish as among the non-Irish, that my confessing to it will seem the merest perverse bravado. Did not Austin Clarke, did not James Joyce before him, dedicate a lot of their time to castigating just this proclivity in Irish society in their lifetimes, and to forcing Irish readers to confront facts of sexuality that the prudish proprieties of their society refused to acknowledge? Yes, both Clarke and Joyce did this; and so far as I am concerned this aspect of their endeavours is the most boring thing about both of them. Joyce's *Ulysses* is a great book; but it is also a smutty and sniggering book, and the worse for that. And in Clarke's last poems, what had once been a hearty bawdry has become the merest pornography.

I touch here on what I have constantly experienced as the widest and least passable gulf between myself and those English-speaking contemporaries with whom on other matters I feel most in common. I am, and have always been – let's face it – a prude. 'Let's face it', I say, and am speaking to myself. Let me admit, after nearly sixty years, what I have rather consistently concealed: that I pick my way warily and distrustfully through modern writing because I know from too much experience how likely it is that, if I once stray away even timidly from what I know as beaten paths, I shall find my stomach turned by the recounting in bald print of activities that I either had never dreamed of or else, if I had dreamed of them, had immediately suppressed as improper and unclean. I have written this in a poem; but on this as on other matters I now spell it out in prose because I have too much evidence that nowadays what is said in verse is in important ways not *said* at all.

How challenging, then, as I wait for the Dublin plane in any English airport, to recognize in the nuns and priests among my fellow-travellers (so drearily commonplace as those priests are, compulsive smokers of cigarettes, dandruff on their collars) the evidence of chastity as a persistently available way of life! To be sure, it is not available to me; and to be sure, the way of chastity may be rather more professed than practised – but I rule out those shameful though inescapable protestant fantasies about how, beginning with masturbation, those papist religious in fact 'manage'! I suppress too those too ready and glib correlations between sexual abstinence and alcoholic indulgence, how the Irishman would rather chase a bottle than a skirt.

At all events I can't fail to record how deep-seated in me is this aversion to the 'sexy', how far it reaches back in my experience. Martin Boyd I recall, an author I think Australian and now forgotten, and doubtless tame enough in all conscience if I were to peruse him now, as I did in the back garden in Dodworth Road in my late teens. You must not say I was 'shocked' by his 'explicitness'; you must say that my stomach was turned, for the reaction was as visceral as that. I remember feeling the same when, at about the same time in my life, I read some D. H. Lawrence; I felt – this seems to be the right word – *affronted*. And that same mutinous recoil, 'affront', is what I have experienced time and again over the years, what I expect to feel (and am seldom proved wrong) whenever, exhausted and looking only for relaxation, I pick up a novel by a contemporary. Edna O'Brien is one instance that I have experienced, out of doubtless many more, and more outrageous: 'How *dare* she,' I furiously ask myself, 'when she promises entertainment, only turn my stomach over?' Kingsley Amis, my favourite novelist among my British peers, earns my gratitude by rather consistently taking me to the point where I think I am going to heave in nausea, but then at the crucial point just sparing me – chiefly because, so far as I can see, he never forgets that sex, producing though it does both woes and exaltations, is yet in the last analysis *comical*; but also because, almost alone among our innumerable 'explicit' authors, he acknowledges and values the tenderness that ennobles decent sexual relations even at their most farcical.

And yet, these being in truth my feelings about sexuality in literature, I seem to be all on my own – unless indeed the admirable Mrs Mary Whitehouse has marshalled some who are of my way of feeling. There are, it seems – and among those I am happy to call my friends – some who are positively entertained by Edna O'Brien or by, to take another very troubling case, Donald Thomas's widely acclaimed *The Flute-Player*. Oh yes, yes, of course one knows the states of mind and feeling in which sexual desire is so imperious that it dominates the entire conscious life, germinating fantasies the more extreme and grotesque according as the need becomes more desperate. And yes, yes, of course one knows the unparalleled happiness when desire can be gratified, especially in ways which earn it the name of 'love'. True too that it's cheating to make much of the exaltation of desire become love, without attending also to the painful and farcical extremities of desire unsatisfied. But I am less confused about this than I used to be. For I have come to see clearly that there is no way to reconcile the essential and precious privacy of the amorous life, with the unavoidable publicity of print. Or rather there is indeed one way, and of course it is the time-honoured way; by euphemism, which is to say circumlocution, which is to say figurative language. This is what makes Yeats, not Joyce nor Austin Clarke, the most erotic of Irish writers. The handful of poems that he wrote for his wife under the figure of King Solomon addressing the Queen of Sheba are more audacious, under the thinly transparent but necessary veil more 'outspoken', even (if it comes to that) more titillating, than the most notorious passages of *Ulysses* or the most outlandish late poems by Clarke. When Yeats read *Lady Chatterley's Lover* he said that each of the famous four-letter words was like a hole burned in the page; and in saying so he voiced no prissy constraint, but was rather making a technical point, surprised to see so practised a writer as Lawrence falling into a novice's trap, trying to take an impossible short cut. The earlier Lawrence had known better, though his figures for the sexual encounter are never so surprising, so compact, or so just as Yeats's. And indeed Lawrence knew all about the need for privacy; in *The Forsyte Saga*, he said with furious distaste, men and women couple as unconcernedly as dogs in the street. Just so, or maybe so; but a page of print is as public as any street-corner, tramped over by as many heedless or coarse or innocent eyes, unless the writer's tact and invention can turn it into a bedchamber, screened from the street by the lace-curtain of metaphor. In those still more public places, the theatre-stage and the cinema or television screen, only the enacted metaphors of dance can effect the transformation – as Yeats recognized after Pound had shown him the Noh plays, and he saw in them the use of hieratic gesture and movement.

This is not a sophisticated argument. No step in it is either difficult or new. My parents and my parents-in-law, if it had been explained to them, would have decided impatiently that it went without saying. How then have we got into a situation where we cannot pick up a book or a magazine, nor switch on the television, without suffering the products of a fatuously more naive understanding of the connection between our experiences (not just our sexual experiences) and the images that we make of them? The *naiveté* is assumed, it is wilful; none of the producers, and few of the consumers, are deceived by their own appeals to a long exploded and never respectable understanding of 'realism'. And thus the phenomenon is vicious, not in its effects, but in origin and in principle. Sex on the screen – apparently naked man on apparently naked woman; gruntings; jerkings – can be devised and defended only by Joseph Brodsky's *literati*, 'not from the desire for truth but from the intellectual smugness of slavery'. And sure enough it is our *literati* – the British more impudently than the Americans, leave alone the Russians – who in newspaper columns and schoolrooms apply themselves to emptying the word 'decency' of all meaning, as of all connection with 'decorum'.

Douglas Brown died before he and his homosexual fellows began to be exhorted to 'come out of the closet'. If he had survived to hear this call, I'm not sure how he would have responded, for he was generally well-disposed to causes that could present themselves as 'progressive'. (If he embraced them however, for instance in education, his tough-mindedness promptly subverted them from within.) But he was an ascetic, and I'm sure would have mortified his flesh just as fiercely if he had been 'straight'. As he was careful to condone homosexual practices 'for those who felt the need of them', so I dare say he would have approved of 'Gay Liberation' for those who felt the need of *that*. But we had among our friends homosexuals whom we had every reason to think of as 'practising'. And I think he would have been pained if these had declared themselves. (So far as I know, they have not.) For he would have agreed that, if by 'closet' we mean a room with a locked door and a curtained window, then a closet is the right place for sexual overtures and encounters, whatever the sexes involved. In other words flamboyance is as distasteful from the gay as from the straight; and indecent exposure isn't limited to what is recognized as such by a law-court.

On the other hand I'm not sure he would have agreed with me that sex is from most points of view comic. He might have thought that one called it that so as not to admit that it was disturbing. But of course disturbing is what it is, as it is also noble or tragic or elevating, at all events serious, when seen in and through the eyes of the lovers – unless of course both have entered on it as a brutally squalid transaction from the first. But comic is all it can be, and *the best* it can be, from every other point of view. For every other point of view is through the keyhole, a public view of an essentially private act; and comedy is the best one can make of that incongruity.

But what is one to do with that specially broad and licensed keyhole, the missing fourth wall of the proscenium stage? The hieratic or otherwise stilted conventions of Yeats's drama, in different ways of Beckett's and Pirandello's, and of most drama before the eighteenth century, makes no pretence of the fourth wall; but in a realistic drama which makes that pretence and depends on it, what we experience in the theatre is certainly the illusion of eavesdropping. And about all this Douglas was in two minds: although he was deeply suspicious of the circles round the Cambridge dramatic societies, yet he would not miss any of their productions, and I remember enduring by his side in the Arts Theatre O'Neill's *Long Day's Journey into Night* – a longer and more tedious journey, as I experienced it, than even that self-indulgent playwright can have intended; similarly, when he returned to the Perse as a schoolmaster, Douglas inherited from Caldwell Cook's day a special experimental theatre called 'the Mummery', and staged productions there before invited audiences. Must he not have acted there himself, if only to show his schoolboy actors what he expected of them? Remembering the neat grace with which he inhabited his body and steered its movements, I think he would have enjoyed that, and done it well. And yet to another part of himself any sort of play-acting was deeply suspect and distasteful. Flamboyance, even sexual flamboyance – it must have more rights than Douglas or I (for I partly shared his ambivalence) could find room for. During my first years in Trinity I had difficulty coping with the innate histrionics of the Anglo-Irishman, grumbling that one after another of my best students came to speak of literature only in the accents and the vocabulary of the green-room.

Douglas would have concurred with me in that. And yet I am forced to recognize that the actor in Douglas went deep and lived very near the heart of him. My son Mark reminds me that he knew Douglas best as a scoutmaster, and testifies that Douglas played that role to the hilt, in no way backing off from the element of fancy dress that it let him in for. For instance at the annual summer camp near West Runton 'the campfire' was not anything that was simply allowed to happen each night when darkness fell; on the contrary, on the three or four nights set aside in the fortnight for this ritual, a rite was indeed what Douglas made of it, donning a ceremonial robe (doubtless only a blanket with a pattern sewn on it in coloured cloth) and inaugurating the proceedings with an exordium in set terms, concluding: 'Brother Scouts, the campfire is open.' For that matter, as my son remarks, Douglas adopted with equanimity, even with a sort of zest, all the quaintly Edwardian language and harmless flummery of Baden-Powell's *Scouting for Boys*, even though he would have been the first to entertain seriously (until he could reject it in good conscience) the allegation commonly heard that Baden-Powell had invented a para-military organization. My own guess is that in this matter Douglas's histrionism and his authoritarianism came together; for certainly he *commanded* his troop of Boy Scouts, insisting very meticulously on hierarchies and chain of command, so that his 14-year-old patrol-leaders experienced as an awesome responsibility their elevation to the 'Court of Honour' to which he summoned them individually, each by plain postcard bearing the summons impersonally and formally typed on his italic-face typewriter. Do I make too much of this – of the phenomenon of 'the born actor', and Douglas Brown as an instance of the type? Not in my own sense of the matter; for what it enforces is the perception that in the actor's art, as in other performing and also creative arts, rigour and restraint may be of the essence – hence that the puritan and the artist are by no means, as is too commonly supposed, at loggerheads. And if, as is doubtless true, Douglas's devotion to his schoolboys was at bottom an erotic interest, it was his puritanism that compelled and enabled him to sublimate it into something useful and even artistic – the art of the dedicated pedagogue.

Nowadays what I see, riding in the Dublin airport coach to Store Street through the predictable grimy rain, is Eros indeed acknowledged in each of the suburban concrete cubes of cohabitation, yet at the same time frowned upon by the frequent, massive and unbeautiful churches. This sends me the message that Eros is a power indeed, and a dangerous one – not a joker in the pack, but rather a knave. A face-card certainly, yet the least eminent of them, useful mainly for frustrating the overweening designs of kings and queens and aces, not to speak of bullying priests. I know what it is to rebel at this, times when I want Love to trump any ace in the pack; and we were angry and indignant when in 1956 or 1957 a Roman Catholic had married a Protestant in Fethard-on-Sea, and a priest, backed by a bigoted community, drove the young couple to selling their farm and emigrating to Canada. That story in the newspapers had something to do with our being ready to leave Ireland when the chance came, even though we had found Dublin very congenial and a good place to rear children in. And yet the Irish attitude has at least this traditional truth about it – that inside or outside wedlock, Eros is often a woefully or else astringently comical power, constantly muddling and derailing thoughts about, and aspirations towards, 'higher things'. I need no one to tell me, however, how poor a thing life would be, without him!

It is always a toil, from Store Street bus-station to Trinity. It is too short a distance for a taxi-cab. And yet, suitcase in hand, one must labour across open spaces and the whirl of circling traffic to the Liffey quays and so across Butt Bridge, wind-whipped likely enough; only then, after another quarter-mile and crossing another thoroughfare, to gain the College Street gate. The quiet that then falls, the gate having closed behind, is worth having struggled for. Trinity is more signally an enclave than any Oxford or Cambridge college, simply because the city hums and snarls all round it as round none of them. There is no university quarter, no Old Aberdeen; the entire quarter, one might say, is enclosed within its walls. A stronghold of Ascendancy privilege, declaring itself so by the ring of its blackened walls, pierced by only three gates? An architectural symbol of the beleaguered state of that Ascendancy, even when most ascendant? Some one must have thought that, and said it; though when we were there nothing was much more touching than the common Dubliner's pride in Trinity, and affection for it, however he was opposed to what it had stood for. When we got there, in 1950, it no longer stood for that, nor to a stranger's eye did it stand for anything else except a long and curious and intermittently glorious past. This has changed. Under Provost Lyons, Trinity has taken on the air of a brisk and thriving, well-cared-for place. I liked it more when its grandeur was somewhat slatternly and

Trinity College Dublin: the front square

unkempt. Over the years I have thought and said that the affection we invested in Trinity was the special sort reserved for the casualty of history, the home of a lost cause; but it would be insufferable to regret that the casualty has returned to the firing line, and found a new cause to replace the lost one. However, when Trinity was gaunt its grandeur was more plainly architectural than now, amid trim flower-beds, shaven

D.D., Fellow of Trinity College Dublin, 1954

lawns and re-set cobblestones. What is pictured on all the postcards, the facade looking on to College Green, I have always thought rather meanly proportioned, and the statues of Burke and Goldsmith that flank the Main Gate, though I thrill to their symbolic rightness, are in truth rather *dumpy*. But the Front Square which opens before you as you pass through the gate has a lofty spaciousness surpassing even the Great Court of the other Trinity, in Cambridge. And the rooms behind are as nobly proportioned as the facades promise. When I was made a Fellow in 1954, I was given one of those rooms, up a single flight of stairs in Front Square. It has gone now, quite properly partitioned to provide student chambers and the washrooms that in my day were few and hard to find. It was gaunt and grand and dirty. When we attended receptions in the late afternoons, we would leave our two small children there, and return to find them in the Yorkshire phrase 'black-bright' with the soot they had picked up from tables and chairs and the vast window-ledges. Infrequently and without conviction I would expostulate with the college-servant, Larry; and at least once that ex-milkman replied: 'Ah well now, sorr, but ye must admit I look after yez and Mrs Davie when ye're at the Provost's.' And it was true enough: Larry's delinquencies with duster and wash-cloth were made good in the Provost's sherry, when he did duty as a waiter and his blotched high-coloured face hovered attentively over our glasses.

The room was full of soot because it was warmed only by an open coal-fire, which I would find roaring up the chimney when I arrived on a winter morning. One morning about ten o'clock, when I was disgrace-fully enough drinking sherry by myself before that fire, a stranger knocked at the door and introduced himself as Padraic Fallon, whose poems I had read with respect, mostly in *The Dublin Magazine*, a long-established and old-fashioned quarterly edited by Seumas O'Sullivan. Fallon's poems were never collected until after his death, and then at-tracted much less attention than they deserve. He was no Trinity man, but a Customs official down in Wexford. Seated and supplied with sherry, he asked about the book in my lap – which was, as I showed him, an anthology out of which I would in forty minutes or so lecture to the Pass class, that is to say, to future lawyers and physicians (for Trinity's Ordinary Degree was required of those who would enter the professional schools, and a very good thing too). That morning, I explained, I would lecture on Shakespeare. 'Ah', said Fallon, 'well ye can't tell 'em of course, but y'know it wasn't him at all.' 'No?' I queried. 'Ah no', he said, "twas Manners y'know. John Manners, Earl of Rutland.' He was thoroughly affable about it. Unforeseeable and inconsequential, such encounters happen to me only in Dublin.

A collegiate university with only one college, Dublin seems to me just

the right size for a university, both physically and in other ways. Physically, T.C.D. is 'a campus', more truly so than those American universities I know, where the so-called campus sprawls across many city-blocks
and is continually engulfing more. Trinity has walls, is a firmly delimited
territory, amicably in tension with the streets outside. It is physically and
manifestly one whole thing, not a congeries of far-flung or interlocked
departments and institutes. In four centuries it has not outgrown its
original site; and although a new library building and lecture-block has
covered over the always unpeopled Fellows' Garden that I used to cross
on my way to a postern-gate in Nassau Street, there still lie open, between
Front Square and the Natural Science laboratories near the rear gate, the
football field and a cricket field round which on Trinity Monday we would
loiter and parade towards strawberries and cream. For the first and
probably the last time in my life, there in Trinity and for Trinity I felt
faintly that loyalty towards institutions – the regiment, the old school, the
college, the club – which engaged the emotions of my fellow-Englishmen
in a way that for the most part I couldn't comprehend. When we were
there Trinity, we were told, was poor as a church-mouse, and certainly
under steady hostile pressure from sectarian nationalism fanned in the
rival institution, the National University; but there was of course no
question of realizing the assets represented by the *Book of Kells* and the
Book of Durrow and the other ancient *incunabula* held in stewardship for
the nation. That sentiment and that principle could not easily be accommodated in universities I have moved in since, factories producing 'research' and graduates (very much in that order). The false analogy on
which these plume themselves, between their operations and those of
industry, is reflected in their architecture, as Trinity's quite different
conception of itself is mirrored in the pillared porticoes, not all of them
grandiose, which allude insistently to temple and shrine.

Of recent years – by which I mean, heaven help me, the last twenty or
so – the focus of my Irish experience has been not Dublin but Sligo; and
in Sligo, the Imperial Hotel on the riverside street that is still called, or was
until lately, 'the Mall'. Much, oh much of my imaginative life is invested
in that distinctly run-down building. In its bar I have talked with Austin
and Nora Clarke, George and Paddy Fraser, Kathleen Raine and Sonia
Orwell, John and Christine Kelly, Helen Vendler and Barbara Hardy,
John Unterecker and Tom Flanagan, Joe and Cleo Barber, and how many
more! In its dining-room I have recalled with Lorna Reynolds how the
pair of us were once shepherded by a living legend, antiquarian, genealo-
gist and advocate, 'the Pope O'Mahony', into a train for Cork (this
sometime in the mid-1950s, snow falling, from that splendid railway
station up by the Guinness Breweries, which Yeats and Lady Gregory and

Sean O'Casey knew); there too, in the dining-room, I remember Enid Henn presiding, successfully determined – she an Englishwoman, and city councillor of Cambridge – not to be disconcerted by the Irish convivial habits that she had decided in advance (and how gallantly, eyebrows and voice hoisted to a defensive irony she couldn't have defended) to regard as 'amusing'. There too, in what I must still call the coach-yard, I made my farewells to Tom Henn himself, founder of the Yeats Summer School, painfully (with his war-injured hip) hoisting himself into a little car for a week's Connemara fishing after the Summer School was over. There also, in the Imperial Hotel and specifically in its 'writing room', glass-partitioned for the use of commercial travellers who vanished decades ago, I wrote through the early hours, fortified by Guinness every 45 minutes, what I suppose to be the best lectures I have ever given on modern, specifically Yeats's poetry – this, years after Tom Henn was dead, and Enid senile in a Cambridge rest-home, yet done partly for them and in their memory. In its 'residents' lounge', a more precarious refuge because it houses the T.V. set, I have read and annotated Yeats's poems and his *Autobiographies*, and other books, most recently Jack Clemo's *Confessions of a Rebel*. And it was from the Imperial, there beside the fast-running and swan-haunted and waterweed-combing Garravogue, that I set out in a rented car perhaps fifteen years ago through the empty and tufted landscapes of Mayo, to rescue at the desolate railway junction of Claremorris a wife and small son, Doreen understandably near to tears after strikes and other misadventures had dogged their flight from San Francisco to Shannon by way of London. Most memorably, in that hotel's piously over-

Sligo: 'the fast-running and swan-haunted and waterweed-combing Garravogue'

furnished 'Yeats room', I have sung and read and recited, laughed and gesticulated and shouted, until three or four in the morning. On one occasion, I am told, Tom Henn appeared to reprove the revellers, dressing-gowned but in other respects every inch the brigadier that he had been in World War Two. It is likely enough; no more in Sligo than in Cambridge could Tom effectively get together the three aspects of himself – as Anglo-Irishman, British Army officer, and Cambridge don. His attempts to do so were not always comical, but sometimes desperate and brave, as when from his deep-dyed and long superannuated Unionist standpoint he harangued a public audience – there, in Sligo – on the shortcomings of the Irish Republic as seen through a Yeatsian's eyes. He was heard out with courtesy – which says much for the civility of his republican audience; but the occasion does him credit too, for quite properly he refused to let the great dead poet be safely interred in seminars and seminar-papers and commentaries, insisting instead that his criticisms of the society he lived in still be heard. Now Henn's photograph hangs, handsome in soft focus (for he was a very vain man), on the ground floor of the building by the bridge that the Royal Bank of Ireland has made over to the Yeats Society. And that is right. For whether he knew it or not, he, with the help of his Sligo collaborators like Frank Wynne (whose portrait hangs beside his), made of the annual Yeats Summer School in Sligo a better and more vital memorial than has, so far as I am aware, been instituted for any other modern poet, anywhere, ever. And the late-night laughter and declamations, in the 'Yeats room' or in the Social Centre a quarter-mile away, are crucial to this achievement. At this annual festival, as I suspect at no other that is comparable, after the sufficiently erudite lectures and seminars, the enthusiasm – quite simply, the poetry and the intoxication of it – spills over and becomes the substance or the measure of what people entertain each other with. What an achievement that is! And where else but in Sligo, in the Republic of Ireland, are the much debated gulfs between poetry and life, or poetry and society, effortlessly surpassed, year after year? Few deserve more credit for that than Julia and Aengus, who keep the Imperial Hotel.

It was not always so. On our first visit to Sligo, in the early 1950s, before Tom Henn and Frank Wynne and others had gone to work, we stayed in the Yeats Country Hotel at Rosses Point; and, when I paid my bill, I gestured towards the portrait of the poet which was the only indication given of what gave the hotel its name. 'Was there', I asked, 'much interest shown in it, or in him?' 'Ah no', the young woman assured me, glancing indifferently and rather bemusedly at the picture, 'to be sure there had been, some years ago. But of late it had all blown over rather.' Once over the years since, and yet it must be all of twenty years ago, we stayed at that hotel again, along with Graham Hough – an occasion commemorated by the fact that my copy of Yeats's *Collected Poems* carries Graham's signature, as doubtless his copy carries mine. That was one experiment we made of settling in for the Yeats Summer School elsewhere than in the Imperial; another one, more ambitious, came when we rented a house in Dromahair, County Leitrim – an experience that I much enjoyed, though the rest of my family didn't. I drove in to my duties in Sligo around the hauntingly beautiful and unpeopled shores of Lough Gill – heavenly! And Ed Dorn with his family came from Essex to join us. With the Dorns we drove – this was in the 1960s – for a day into Donegal, in glorious weather (rare at that north-western extremity of Ireland, yet for us unfailing, as on two holidays we spent at Inver, northward from Sligo). Give the Irish Tourist Board much credit; at the entrance to Dromahair from the west stands a sign that gives in full the poem by Yeats where Dromahair is mentioned, 'The Man Who Dreamed of Fairyland'. And a few miles away, where one parks the car to climb to the waterfall of Glencar, there is a similar sign with the appropriate poem once again given in full. I think there is a similar notice-board out there on the coast, at the entrance to the bald and heart-breaking house of the Gore-Booths, Lissadell, under Ben Bulben:

> The light of evening, Lissadell,
> Great windows open to the south,
> Two girls in silk kimonos, both
> Beautiful, one a gazelle . . .

The windows are not 'great', and the house is by no means grand, nor is it well-tended. But that is just the point, and the poignancy; a poet's gift of golden language has lifted it past Blenheim and Monticello into an image of ultimate opulence and refinement, simply by virtue of the most triumphantly audacious rhyme in modern English, 'Lissadell' with 'gazelle'. The rhyme makes it, makes everything, even to a landmark on the foreign tourist's itinerary. How can poets, and the readers of poetry, not cherish a country where this can happen? I cannot answer for Ed Dorn; but for my part I recall these images with a quite outrageous wistfulness and hunger.

Shall I be told that the adolescent psychopaths who carry guns and bombs for the I.R.A. are no less products and representatives of the country whose capital is Dublin? That is a lie; most citizens of the Republic hate and fear the I.R.A. terrorists as much as the British do, or the Ulster Protestants. To be sure (and the best of them will acknowledge it) there is something shamefully duplicitous about their government's conduct towards these assassins, a policy directed always towards ensuring that they shoot at British soldiers, not soldiers of the Republic. And to be sure – a more damaging and distressful admission – there are to be found in Anglo-Irish poetry, not least in Yeats's, passages which may seem to condone and even invite their atrocities. For saying as much, and acting on it while he was Minister in an Irish government, the most courageous of Irish politicians, Conor Cruise O'Brien, has been hounded from office, and brought down with him his party's government. But what does all this amount to, even in the eyes of an indignant Englishman like myself, beyond the fact that poetry, even in the hands of a civically responsible poet (and Yeats to be sure was not so responsible as he might have been), is *dynamite*, an explosive substance which can work on the mind of the half-educated so as to wreak atrocious havoc? Who, that knows even a little about poetry, ever doubted this? And who, that cares for poetry, would wish it otherwise? This stuff (poetry) is dangerous and double-edged; if it were not so dangerous, would we spend so much time trying to learn how to handle it?

For many years, under Tom Henn but also under others of the early 'directors', the effective centre and resident sage of the Yeats Summer School was Oliver Edwards, Anglo-Welshman but Anglo-Irish by adoption, from Magee College in Derry, who laboured under the bizarre and unforeseeable disadvantage of having by baptism the name which an editor of *The Times* ('greatest newspaper in the world', as I write extinguished by its labour unions) would adopt as a nom-de-plume. Oliver had known Yeats, and had from him in conversation *aperçus* which mysteriously Oliver was never able to convey into print. Clean-shaven and lean and smallish and ruddy-jowled, like a less saturnine Austin Clarke, Oliver I take it disguised in low-voiced tomfoolery at his own expense what may have been a quite searing smart at his inability to purvey his considerable and curious learning, in German literature as well as Anglo-Irish. In 1969, when I had published in *The Irish Times* a poem called 'Ireland of the Bombers', in which I had shaken the dust of Ireland from my feet because of I.R.A. atrocities against the innocent ('Blackbird of Derrycairn/Sing no more for me . . .'), Oliver, nationalist though he was and protestant, wrote accepting the blame: '*our* disgrace'. Just so, some years later (it must have been 1975), when Augustine Martin, a Senator of the Republic, wrote asking me to resume my connections with the Yeats Summer School, he took note of my poem: 'Despite what you have written . . .' Is there another country in the English-speaking world where the publication of a poem in a periodical is taken so seriously, taken such note of, where the asseverations one makes in a poem are taken so much in earnest? If not, small wonder that we poets and enthusiasts for poetry nurse for this country, Ireland, a love not at odds with our several patriotisms, but enriching those and complicating them, sometimes painfully.

At any rate no country has treated its great poet so handsomely as, though somewhat belatedly, Ireland has treated Yeats. One acknowledges the Chamber of Commerce argument that it is good for business. If it is, who will begrudge the Sligo tradesman the few extra pounds or dollars that the connection brings him? And in any case in places like Dromahair the Irish tourist industry seems only modestly and inconspicuously more thriving than it was twenty years ago. Nor does one notice in Ireland any need to drag the father down, to make room for aspiring sons and daughters. In the 1970s, when the poets who visited the Sligo school came less from Dublin than from 'the North' (James Simmons, Michael Longley, Paul Muldoon), Jimmy Simmons in particular, troubadour of those tormented years, seemed far more aware than other such minstrels I have known of how the requirements of the art of poetry persist, as it must seem to some unfeelingly, unchanged and unaffected by the understandably heated emotions of any convulsed present. For Jimmy Simmons those requirements were embodied in – what else? – the poems of Yeats.

8

Californians

It was from Dublin that I first went to America. In the suburban small house that we had at Raheny, on the unfashionable north side of Dublin Bay, Hugh Kenner had come to stay during the first days of his first visit to Europe. And that was instructive too; I think of it as the most telling evidence I've ever had, of how sheerly informative literature can be. For Hugh had already written his *Dublin's Joyce*. And I remember, as I drove us into the city on a rainy overcast morning through Killester and Clontarf, telling Hugh where he was, and hearing him respond with satisfaction, 'Ah yes – it is just as I imagined.' He was right too; as he was later, when I and Sean White took him to Dublin Castle and the Dolphin chophouse, and to other places. He possessed Dublin already, inside his head, from reading Joyce; its topography, and the social or psychological resonance of that topography. All he sought was confirmation; and he sought it without anxiety, so sure he was of the imaginative possession that his author had given him – with an assurance that was vindicated, as he knew it would be. He was so sure of the truthfulness of Joyce's imagination that he could extrapolate from things that Joyce had said or implied, to predict with accuracy things which Joyce had not told him about, even by implication. He knew, for instance – and of course quite rightly – that, leaving aside a few freakish instances, Dublin possessed no Romantic architecture, no Scottish-baronial or Victorian Gothic; that in that art, as in literature and oratory, the Romantic Revival had passed Ireland by – so that modestly good suburban building was in Dublin, as late as the 1860s, still recognizably in a classical idiom.

Hugh, it turned out, was looking for someone to replace him in the University of California at Santa Barbara, during a year's sabbatical leave that he meant to spend in his native place, in and about London, Ontario. It was harder for me to find a replacement at Trinity. But I succeeded. And so in the summer of 1957 we sailed for New York on the *Britannic* out of Liverpool.

My own contact in the U.S.A., specifically in California, was a man whose declared interests and sympathies had turned him far away from that constellation of modernists – Pound and Eliot, Yeats and Wyndham Lewis and Joyce – which stood at the zenith for Hugh Kenner. This man was Yvor Winters, whom I had discovered for myself before 1950, borrowing from the Cambridge Union what may at that date have been the one copy of *In Defense of Reason* to be found in the British Isles. I had written to Winters with admiring enthusiasm, and there had ensued some talk of my joining the faculty at Winters's university, Stanford – an idea which was translated into fact only twenty years later, when Winters was dead.

Winters . . . This paradoxical person, great doctor of abstractions in his own verse and when he discussed the verse of others, gave the impression, when one met him, of lifting a heavy boot with immense difficulty out of a tangle of the earthiest particulars. What passed for conversation with him was a ruminative and halting monologue about the behaviour of Canadian waxwings when they migrated southward over his home in Los Altos, or the multiple nice distinctions within the botanical family

D.D. and Janet Lewis Winters on the porch of Yvor Winters's house, Los Altos

that includes the great madrone; or else, though this pleased him less as it embarrassed us more, the three best poems (in order) by that under-rated poet Robert Bridges, the three most over-rated poems by that overrated author, W. B. Yeats.

It was, I now realize, apprehension more than his corpulence, which had him walking towards me with an exaggerated rolling, down the railroad tracks in the sunshine of Santa Barbara. His small travelling-bag swung from his hand with an unhappy excess of assumed carelessness, and he glared at me mistrustfully through strong lenses. What a conquest it was of his mistrust, thus to have lured him so far afield (for he judged 200 miles of distance by a European, not a Californian scale), I had been made to realize before he came, and indeed had had some sense of eight years before, when the brisk interchange of letters between us had rather awkwardly lapsed. I knew with how much suspicion – to begin with, not unfounded – he regarded the literary and academic world outside his home campus, let alone east of the Rockies; and could imagine how little he knew what to make of a phenomenon such as myself, from east of the Atlantic, that sea he had never crossed. That I was a professed admirer was, to a person of his delicacy, hard enough; that I should be an admirer very jealous of my own independence complicated things a little more.

For with a temerity that now surprises me, with what must have looked like a coolly deliberate showing of my hand, I had heralded a visit to his home-ground, to stay with old friends Wes and Helen Trimpi, by publish-ing a review of the latest product of Winters's small but distinguished poetic stable, Edgar Bowers's *A Form of Loss*. I had written of it admiringly, yet with rather stern qualifications; and had gone out of my way, almost, to demur at Winters's enthusiastic estimate. When the Winterses came to dine with the Trimpis, they brought with them Thom Gunn, whom I had looked forward to meeting hardly less than to meeting them. I thought the disagreement about Bowers had to be brought into the open; so I broached the subject after dinner, and Winters and I ex-changed some half-dozen fiercely civil sentences about it. If I had not done this I think he might not have agreed later in the evening to consider coming to Santa Barbara and giving a public reading of his poems.

What I liked most about Winters's poetry was just the side of him that numbered the botanical relations of the madrone, on which very subject, in fact, he has a sombre and mysteriously evocative short poem. Better still to my mind are some poems of his, such as 'John Sutter' or 'California Oaks' or 'A View of Pasadena from the Hills', in which a Californian landscape, regarded with just this particularizing intentness, intersects with, or leads into, some chapter of Californian history. And if I had felt

San Francisco

this when I read his poems in Europe, I felt it all the more after I had reached California; not just, hardly at all in fact, because the literary record could then be measured against the reality, but because I saw how rare in California is such a sense of history, the sense of a past pressed up close behind the present, conditioning it. This awareness is so much a need of any imaginative European that people who lack it, however rich their personalities in other ways, and however nimble their minds, must seem to him to lack a necessary human dimension. The ache of that absence, I am sure, persists in us of the Old World, however long we may live in California. At any rate the Winterses were toughly and sharply aware of the conditioning past to a degree that would be rare, and refreshing, wherever one encountered it, in the Old World or the New. Janet Winters, as I later came to know her through her books, was even more than her husband a case in point.

As for Santa Barbara, its history had been obliterated in a typically Californian way, by having an elaborately fabricated false past laid on top of the true one. Its main street shaken down by an earthquake in the twenties, the chance had been seized, by the retired wealth which was already taking it over, to rebuild the city in a Spanish style in keeping with its name. The result, though not at all authentic, was beautiful; the little city began to measure up to the grandeur of its natural setting, and I distrust the antiquarian nostalgia in myself which would persuade me that such wholesale transformations are always wrong. Certainly, though, the re-building had the effect of removing authenticity from the one or two buildings that did in fact survive from the Spanish period – a couple of adobe dwellings, a guard-house, and the Franciscan 'mission'. What had happened to the mission buildings was particularly significant: trimmed, re-pointed and varnished to earn the accolade, 'Queen of the Missions', it had lost, like Carmel northward in the chain, all that ability to stir the imagination which survived for instance in the more remote foundation at Santa Ynez, still gaunt and allowed its evidence of time's erosions, in the torrid and sparsely peopled valley of the Santa Ynez river behind the coastal range. (Santa Ynez, alas, has also been 'prettified' lately.) Winters, though himself no 'native son', served as memorialist of Los Angeles as of San Francisco and Sacramento; and his talk of a relative who was first to inhabit Eagle Rock – an indistinguishable suburb now, between Los Angeles and Pasadena – went along with his reminiscences of mining-camps in New Mexico, and a journey forty years before from there to Idaho. Before his baleful gaze, determined to bite upon historical fact, Santa Barbara – so spick and span, with its cool patios and fountains – withered back into the dusty outpost that Richard Henry Dana knew.

112

Nine years later I was in Stanford again, and not on a flying visit but for six weeks on end. It was the last summer of Winters's life, and he and his friends guessed as much. Sick and oppressed, he moved heavily about the small house where Janet still lives, pouring whisky for me though it was mid-afternoon. We were alone in the house, and I do not pretend that I was ever at ease with him. In particular, now that he was near the end of his tether, his judgments on poets were more intemperate and seemingly exasperated than ever before. The last thing I wanted was a deadlock of opinions, a clash of wills; and yet equally I could not pretend to concur in his judgment for instance of Wordsworth. On poets and poetry the common ground between us had by this time narrowed to vanishing-point, as his last and posthumous book was to show. Carefully therefore I had selected my topic in advance: Thomas Hardy, whose poems I knew that he still admired, as I did too.

But of course, as I should have foreseen, it didn't work. What poems by Hardy were we supposedly agreeing about? Playing safe as I thought, and rejoicing in Johnsonian phrase to concur with the common reader, I named 'The Voice'. Wrong! Wrong! Typical of 'you professors' – what did he think he was? I wondered – that, faced with two poetic treatments of the same theme, we should infallibly pick the wrong one, the slight one. Much better than 'The Voice' was its companion-piece, 'The Haunter'. Was there ever a champion of the aphorism, the abstract proposition, the generalized maxim, who descended so relentlessly to particulars? Wretched, aggrieved, mortified, I had to say that I didn't know the poem or didn't remember it. In silence he rose, lumbered from the room, and returned with two copies of Hardy's *Collected Poems*. One for him, one for me. The poem was on page 324. I turned to the page, glanced at the poem, realized I didn't know it, and read it, in a subdued voice, aloud. Then promptly, to forestall argument, I asked for the next in the canon according to Winters. He told me, with the page number. That one I read; and then the next; and the next . . . after a while, as the silence became more pregnant between one reading and the next, I asked if he minded this impromptu, unrehearsed performance. No, he replied slowly, he didn't mind. In fact . . . my English accent took him back. It seemed he was hearing again his grandmother reading to him as a child.

I had heard of her once before; she came from Devon, from near Exeter. And in due course I heard, in his growling ruminative monotone, of other figures from his past. But what launched him on this was, appropriately, the last in the canon, 'Afterwards':

> When the Present has latched its postern behind
> my tremulous stay . . .

Bearing in mind that my hearer had never visited England to see what had happened to it, and thinking also (I must confess) how little room is left in Winters's professed view of things for the irrational powerful feelings that tie a man to his native ground, I had ventured a lame enough reflection – how to an English reader a poem like 'Afterwards' had a specially bitter poignancy, seeing that so many of the pastoral landscapes which the poem summoned up had been desolated and expunged since Hardy's day. And he replied, in a gruff mutter, that his own 'View of Pasadena from the Hills' dealt with an analogous despoiling, not just of landscape but of the history which that landscape embodied – a double cancellation, or erasure.

So the readings were over. And Winters began, haltingly, on chapters from his family history. The woman from Devon was his maternal grandmother, an emigrant to Canada, who either in Canada or Michigan met and married his grandfather, impoverished cadet of a gentry family from Schleswig-Holstein (who had emigrated, I think he said, to evade conscription into the Prussian army). This grandfather died young and violently, following amputation by a circular saw; and the grandmother brought up a family of many daughters and one son. This one maternal uncle, who later emigrated to Riverside, California, Winters esteemed and remembered with affection, though he had lacked the practical

Mattei's Tavern, Los Olivos, Santa Barbara County

intelligence he needed for his vocation as farmer. He was accordingly looked down on by his sisters who, trained as schoolmistresses, all found moneyed husbands in or about Chicago. Winters's mother, whom he remembered without much affection, found and married one of two sons of a union between an Orangeman from Ulster (the original American Winters) and a woman from Somerset, Winters's paternal grandmother,

Santa Ynez at dawn: 'prettified lately'

whom he recalled as vulgar and shallow – both epithets were his – yet not without a good heart, and not to be taken lightly.

There was a good deal more, chiefly about Winters's father, and how he bought himself membership in the Chicago 'Board of Trade'. I do not remember any of that. Nor do I remember how I took my leave, though it must have been with a paper sack full of the Santa Rosa plums that he took such pride in, from his little orchard. And I don't remember, either, how I felt as I drove away through that worst despoliation of all, the once Royal Road, *el Camino Real*, now an unbroken strip of kitsch and honky-tonk from San Francisco to San Jose. In any case, memory's not to be trusted. And yet it still seems to me that I had participated in some sort of testamentary disposition of intangible goods, made by an agnostic under the suitably agnostic auspices of Thomas Hardy. It is at any rate small wonder if I do not recognize, in the blurred and touching figure that memory brings back to me, the trenchant polemicist whose pronouncements still provoke heated demonstrations for and against (mostly against) in books and hard-hitting essays.

Another presence known abstractedly in Europe, which took body in the California of 1957, was Waclaw Lednicki. In Murmansk and Archangel in 1942–3 I had picked up a smattering of Russian, and I tried to improve it after the war in Cambridge. I failed; and ever since, my Slavic interests –

Outside Castroville

Polish later, as well as Russian – have been an embarrassment to me, since they are perforce unscholarly. But at the same time they have brought me many advantages; for the world of Slavic scholarship has shown me more generosity than the world of the Anglicists. Among those advantages I certainly count the chance of knowing Lednicki.

I saw him long before I met him, when in the late 1940s he gave some lectures in Cambridge. At that time I was still trying to make something of my Russian, and remember being repeatedly out-distanced as I tried to follow him through a lecture given in Russian on Pushkin's prose. Later I read some of his essays, in French or his execrable written English, on Polish and Russian literature; and so I already knew him as the best historian of Russian literature outside Russia when, years later, I reviewed for *The New Statesman* his *Russia, Poland, and the West*.

The review pleased him greatly, because he was seldom reviewed except in specialist journals. And he wrote to me from the University of California at Berkeley, where he was spending his last professional years after earlier appointments in Cracow and Brussels. There was desultory correspondence after that, abortive plans to meet on his trips to Europe, an equally abortive plan to celebrate the Mickiewicz centenary in Dublin as elsewhere, and some exchange of off-prints. What won me to him was his readiness to accept the terms on which, knowing no Polish, I was putting over into English verse some fragments of the *Pan Tadeusz* of Mickiewicz; and this although he had a deserved notoriety for severity in reviewing professional colleagues, and, as I came to find, a strict sense of scholarly punctilio, so that he could not for instance forgive Vladimir Nabokov for never or seldom acknowledging the contributions of other scholars. This charmed me, and extended my views. For I had been trained in the Cambridge of F. R. Leavis never to speak or think the words 'scholarship' or 'scholarly', except inside mocking or rancorous quotation-marks. I believed that these words represented a patented subterfuge by which the timorous, the malicious and the obtuse could duck away from the really testing questions about literature, particularly questions of value. This wounded me, for I knew myself to possess the omnivorous instincts of at least one kind of scholar. Yet heaven knows I found plenty of evidence, everywhere I turned, that the pretensions of scholarship were indeed as hollow as this. In print I had met, now and again, scholarship that was better; I met it immediately only when Lednicki, quite unflurried by any ambiguity in my amateur status, asked me to contribute to the international centenary symposium on Mickiewicz which he was to edit for the university press at Berkeley. What I was encountering for the first time was a fiercely rigorous scholar whose interests were genuinely in literary history, in literature as a pattern of

117

creative achievements, not as an occasion for the extrication of philologi-
cal niceties or the biographer's impertinence. I was meeting too, and
liking, the full-dress continental solemnity about the world of scholarship, in contrast to the English affectation of the casual and the amateur.
And I think I was meeting too, though this I didn't realize till later, an
equally unEnglish willingness to accord special rights to the poet even
sooner than to the scholar.

I recognized in America the trap into which Dylan Thomas had lately,
tragically, and so notoriously fallen; recognized it so clearly that I was
glad not to have the same temptations, except on the smallest scale,
offered to me. The trap was that debased version of the special rights
accorded to the poet, which permits him – drives him indeed, for the
apparent licence conceals a ruthless resolve to live through him, vicari-
ously – to break through all the social inhibitions which bear heavily on
his avid hosts. What I am remembering now with gratitude is something
older and finer: Rico LeBrun, the grand and veteran painter, with Neapol-
itan ease and elaboration raising his glass in Los Angeles to 'il poeta';
and Lednicki's entertaiment of me in Berkeley.

I was to give two lectures on 'Walter Scott, Mickiewicz and Pushkin'.
People in the English Department – Ian and Ruth Watt, Josephine Miles,
Henry Nash Smith – were very kind to me. Lednicki's kindness had
another edge to it, conveyed as it was through Polish hauteur and formality. He was very neat and ready and alert; almost one could have called
him dapper, except that his manner was too large and composed for that.
He gave an evening party for me at his house, a wholly senior and
masculine gathering where, to begin with, the formality was disconcerting. For as each new guest arrived the conversation, haltingly resumed
after the last arrival, was blocked again by the need for introductions all
round the growing circle. But later, after a supper of Polish dishes with
wine and vodka, I saw the point of the punctilio, and was pierced by it
delightedly. For it was through Lednicki's own writings that I had moved
in imagination into the exquisitely mannered world of Moscow in the
1820s, where Mickiewicz and Pushkin pursued their complicated relationship of affection, aversion and mutual esteem. And there is a famous
anecdotal painting which shows Mickiewicz reciting his poems in the
salon of some aristocratic lady, with Pushkin I believe portrayed among
those who are listening. So now, when Lednicki called for silence so that I
should read my version of Mickiewicz, surprised, gratified, blushing, I
felt a connection between that pictured occasion and this one. Had
Lednicki made the connection, and intended me to make it? Probably
not; to him, I believe, nothing seemed more natural than, when a poet
was being entertained, to ask him to read his poems. And yet only one

other host that I remember has ever made me this gesture; and indeed in the catch-as-catch-can bonhomie of British and American entertaining the gesture would be too formal, not natural at all.

A few months later, when Lednicki came on his summer vacation to Santa Barbara, I had the chance to return his hospitality, and am distressed to think that I did it less than royally. I was at the end of my resources by that time, feeling the strain of an American year that had been as exacting as it was rewarding. I was in no shape to give Lednicki the attention he deserved, and this was a pity because he was feeling at sea himself, retiring from Berkeley, wondering where and how to spend his retirement. This brought home to him what I had seen from the first as part of his melancholy distinction; his exiled solitude here, in the New World. Consciously a European in the way of the educated Pole, yet habituated as only the Pole can be to the condition of exile, he had psychologically speaking never emigrated, never stepped from the shore of the Old World, where indeed – in Poland – I understood there was a daughter unseen for twenty years, and grandchildren never seen at all.

Astonishingly youthful in appearance, trim and softly urbane, discreetly scented and close shaven in a well-pressed linen coat, while in Santa Barbara he took a swim each morning. His loneliness was so far from breaking through his composed courtesy that it was all the harder to refuse to the loneliness what it demanded, a hearing for his insistent and voluble though always measured monologues. Often the hearer was one of a family of his compatriots, the Glinskis, whom we knew already because Teresa, one of the three handsome daughters, was a student on the campus. Her father Tomasz Glinski on his own account delighted me and my office-mate on the campus, Marvin Mudrick: a moneyed playboy (so we gathered) of pre-war Warsaw, he eked out a living by playing the piano for a club in Montecito, the wealthy suburb where a society of similar expatriates, noble and even royal, was said to congregate. Glinski's gaiety and insouciance survived unimpaired into his reduced circumstances; and he took pride, one evening when he helped me through some lines of *Pan Tadeusz*, in having my fingers trace a duelling scar on his scalp.

To get ourselves home from America in 1958, the four of us split into two pairs. My wife's father was dying in England, so she with our daughter, then a five-year-old, flew out of Los Angeles by the polar route – a more remarkable venture then than it has since become; whereas I and my thirteen-year-old son were left to pick our way across the continent so as to pick up our French ship out of New York a month later.

It was the first, and is still the only, journey that I have made otherwise than by air across the continental United States. To Mark and me, as we pulled away from the Greyhound 'bus depot, Santa Barbara waved its goodbye in the person of Ken Millar, whose precariously imperturbable presence has since been revealed to two continents as the identity behind the writer, Ross Macdonald. We rode that day, by way of Los Angeles, to Las Vegas, Nevada; we stayed there, as the four of us had stayed some months before, with one of my wife's cousins, daughter of her father's brother who, Welsh and a shipwright like my father-in-law, had emigrated in the first decade of the century, when the Admiralty's Pembrokeshire dockyard was closed down. Next day, with the thermometer registering over 100, we rode north through the Nevada desert and alighted in Cedar City, Utah. The name meant nothing to me then. It was years later, travelling by train on a summer evening from London to Edinburgh, that I read in Jacob Piatt Dunn's *Massacres of the Mountains* how Cedar City was where the southern route from Salt Lake City to California intersected with the Spanish trail from New Mexico to Los Angeles; and how Cedar City was the base from which in September 1857 Paiute Indians and painted Mormons rode out to exterminate, by 'the will of the Lord', Captain Faucher's train of emigrants from Arkansas. Pleased and bemused by the heat next morning, on an approving stroll through the pastoral outskirts of the little settlement, I had no reason to wonder if there still survived that 'tithing-office at Cedar City', where the bloodied clothes and bedding of Captain Faucher's people lay for weeks after the massacre, and still stank eighteen months later. I was acting and presuming as does every tourist in 'the west', European or American; the west is, by definition, *raw*, it has no history. But it has; those mountain meadows are neither raw nor innocent, their folds have closed over wounds that in some minds suppurate still. The wound that on some supernal map marks Cedar City with a skull had opened and closed before ever my wife's father and his brothers were born in West Wales. The American West is already ancient, in its crimes and in its remorse. Under the manifested copiousness of natural provision there is everywhere a human horror or else a human pathos; even sometimes human responsibility, for Jacob Dunn's indignant accusations of the Whites for what they had done to the Indians were launched as long ago as 1886. But this is something I have learned – and not well enough, not with enough of chapter and verse – only by living there, in the West. In 1958 I was still the European tourist. And the mountain meadow that Mark and I found, on a Union Pacific excursion by coach from Cedar City, was not the scene of that or any other massacre, but the magnificent twenty miles or more of snow-fed grassland that waves on the top of the Kaibab forest as one approaches the North Rim of the Grand Canyon. I have been there since, have driven that exalted road again; and am much less sure now that the meadow is the natural haunt only of porcupine and deer — white men, red men, perhaps black men, seemed on that second visit to be writhing under its tussocks.

9

Italophils

When I look back, the nearer I come in my thoughts to the way that I live now, the harder it is to register as dead some who have moved through life in much the same way as I do still. Douglas Brown and my parents and Yvor Winters; Joe Hone and Lednicki and Austin Clarke – either they died already a long time ago, or else my memories of them belong to a period comfortably past. But William Partridge, whom I remember now, shared with me a world that I think of as still going on: a world of the 1960s, when provincial scholarship boys such as he and I, having modestly 'made it', might experience foreign places more often and more light-heartedly, though also (it must be said) more superficially, than when we struggled abroad on limited funds and lived more cheek-by-jowl with our foreign hosts; the more affluent time when we might arrange on the 'phone to rendezvous in not the worst hotel in King's Lynn; when we could afford to refurbish – slowly, and bit by bit – a weekend home rather like the parental home we had long before grown out of or grown away from; when the populist and egalitarian sentiments that we had adopted as ours, since we had profited by them, rather rapidly turned sour on us as we saw them appealed to for the recognition of 'rights' not earned by any effort; when, the tensions of 'making it' at last relaxed, we were more or less briefly and partially made free of the worlds we had made it into – painting, for him, and poetry, for me.

Either way, the Mediterranean was what we made for. Whatever impelled the other travellers – Belgian or Dutch or German, French or British or American – with whom we barged and hooted down the tourist highways, or jostled at the railway and airport counters, we knew what impelled us, and what drew us: the region where we would throw off our clothes, and learn to live in our skins – not for *dolce far niente* either, but on the contrary for the refining rigours that life under a hot sun would subject us to. Where the shadows were knife-edged, where the sea's colour deepened to indigo, where the torsos were bronzed and the baring of them brazen, where the spray of a fountain was no part of a stage-set but a palpably alleviating presence in a sun-struck plaza – there, as nowhere else in our experience, was the practice of our arts emphatic and masculine, no chasing of fugitive shadows but solid, a manifest statement.

This way of talking about writing was a new one for me, which I encountered, at first suspiciously, sometime in the 1950s. Words like 'manifest' and 'masculine' and even 'solid' were no part of my vocabulary when I was first at Cambridge or had lately left it, nor when I wrote my first books of criticism. It came to me from several sources, of which the only one I can identify with certainty is two books by Adrian Stokes, *The Stones of Rimini* and *The Quattrocento*, which I remember reading, delightedly, on late summer afternoons over a pint of draught Guinness in the bar of The Bailey, in Dublin. That must have been about 1956, some four years after our first brief visit to Italy, and our 'exposure' – the American sophomore's comically clinical word seems here to be the right one – to Mediterranean light, and to how a stand of cypresses or a free-standing sculpture or a facade had to take that light, withstand it, and profit by it. Stokes's art-criticism acknowledged that reality and articulated it, in a way that was impressionistic certainly – what else could it be? – but also, as I found it, disciplined, exact, and moving. At that time I thought he was the only writer of English who did this, though later, re-reading some of D. H. Lawrence's poems from Italy, I saw there was another Englishman who with a different vocabulary had explored the same vivid area. I suspect that my use of this vocabulary of Stokes's, though I have had recourse to it only sparingly, has baffled and sometimes affronted many who otherwise wished me well. And this was true not only of my old Cambridge associates, who would trust no vocabulary but Leavis's, but also of such comrades of 'The Movement' as Kingsley Amis and Philip Larkin.

I yield to hardly anyone in my admiration of Philip Larkin's poetry, and I sometimes see, in his refusal to go for experience outside England, a heroic exploit of self-abnegation beside which my own grabbing for sensuous experience wherever I can find it seems somehow wanton. But I detect in his poetry as a whole, still more in the sort of admiration it elicits from English readers, a drastic and gratuitous contraction of experience for which it still seems to me that the right word is 'Little-Englandism'. The tight little island is nowadays all too proud of its tightness and its littleness. One sees very well that with the dissolution of the Empire, shamefully precipitate as that was, global and imperial vistas would necessarily be closed off for the English imagination. But there has been a wilful contraction far beyond what events dictated, until now patriotism and parochialism are thought to be one and the same. Certainly my friend Philip Larkin did not write his poems according to any such programme, nor to enforce any such state of mind; but his poems have been used by others, and are used by them still, to inculcate just these ignoble attitudes.

Italy: Gemona-del-Friuli, before the earthquake which destroyed it

Nowadays when I observe my native land, whether from far away or on the spot, I feel a sort of despair. For everything I see bears out Solzhenitsyn's and Yuri Orlov's contention: 'even in theoretical terms consistent socialism can take *no other form than the totalitarian*, just as two gears must mesh or an accelerated wheel cannot fail to turn'. I am not being partisan; for it was a Tory minister twenty years ago who declared, with shocking complacency and far more balefully than he knew, 'We are all socialists now'. As Solzhenitsyn has declared further, 'even the mildest methods of introducing socialism, so long as they are consistent and steadfast, can only lead to totalitarianism . . .' It is a necessary condition of such 'consistent and steadfast' indoctrination that the patients to be indoctrinated shall be prevented from measuring up their own experience, as citizens of one State, with the experience of others in other States; and this, which could be effected in the Soviet Union only by systematically excluding information from abroad, can be managed in England by admitting such information but systematically persuading the citizenry to discount it. The poems of Philip Larkin, himself neither socialist nor totalitarian, have been exploited, by 'educators', so as to furnish just such persuasion.

When I inveigh like this against socialism, my friends misunderstand me. I have in mind nothing so circumscribed as a political programme or packet of programmes. Nationalized ownership of industry appears irremediably inefficient, but it does not greatly stir my feelings one way or the other. I take the word 'socialism' seriously, having been compelled to do so by some experiences of the 1960s. It means or it implies – so I was forced to see – that there are no human relations, not even the most intimate, that are not also social. And so for instance under thoroughgoing socialism all the arts must become, as we have seen them become, arts of the *voyeur*, the Peeping Tom, just as the administrator in a socialist state is always the Nosey Parker. For the socialist there are no privileged occasions, no exchanges so private that they cannot be made public. Hence the journalism of the 'revelation' and the 'exposure', the inspired or uninspired 'leak', the supposedly private diary that was always meant for publication. In 1968, as Pro-Vice-Chancellor at Essex, I was flabbergasted to have a junior colleague retail to a mass meeting of many hundreds the substance and the very words of what had passed between us as, I had fondly imagined, private persons. I had been very stupid. Society's claims upon us were to be understood as *total*; privacy henceforth would not be tolerated. Indeed, to have one's privacy invaded, or to cast it away for one's self, was henceforth to be called 'liberation'. And who were to be the liberating and socializing agents? Cameramen, of course; but principally still, and most influentially, word-merchants like myself. With a pang I recognized, among the investigative journalists and self-styled 'satirists' who now rose to fame, the names of men I had taught at Cambridge not many years before. I had been recruiting and training my enemies. And how could I ever have doubted this? Who were the *literati*, if not the men and women who had sat at my feet in Dublin, in Cambridge, and now in Essex? And where had they learned to purvey the half-truth or the irrelevance so plausibly and memorably, with such force, except by study of those truth-telling writers I had set before them? In most people's minds, I came to see, there was self-contradiction involved when a writer, and a teacher of writing, undertook to defend privacy.

I was brought up to think that libertarian principles were so ingrained in the English tradition that in England, if nowhere else, totalitarianism would be quickly unmasked and vigorously resisted. I was taught to take pride in having been born to that strain in the English tradition, the strain of the English Dissenters, in which such promptness and boldness could most be counted on, indeed to excess. But in the last dozen years, since I myself awoke to how state socialism is totalitarian, I have listened in vain for any cheep of protest from the English tradition I am heir to, the tradition of Oliver Cromwell and John Bunyan. And I have accordingly clung the more fondly to the images of individuality that were created, far outside England, by the masterful artificers of Renaissance Italy. Just so, but heroically, did Osip Mandelstam, hounded by Stalin in the 1930s, cling to the witnesses of Dante and Ariosto, obscurely comforting himself by the assurance that the waters of his own Black Sea flowed into and out of the Mediterranean, washing the shores of Italy and Greece. From my North Sea the waterways were altogether more devious and longer. And accordingly I had to overcome several sorts of guarded suspiciousness in myself, and constrictions of sensibility, before the Mediterranean light could bathe and brace and heal. More than twenty-five years ago I put this in a poem which has for epigraph what I remember my mother saying when I was too cocky as a child: 'Mr Sharp from Sheffield, straight out of the knife-box!'

> Americans are innocents abroad;
> But Sharp from Sheffield is the cagey kind
> And – out of the knife-box, bleeding – can't afford
> To bring to Florence such an open mind.
>
> Poor Mr Sharp! And happy transatlantic
> Travellers, so ingenuous! But some
> Are so alert they can finesse the trick,
> So strong they know when to be overcome.

126

Now must he always fall between these stools?
Blind, being keen; dumb, so as not to shrill;
Grounded and ground in logic-chopping schools;
So apt in so inapposite a skill?

Beleaguered and unsleeping sentinel,
He learned the trick of it, before the end;
Saw a shape move, and could not see it well
Yet did not challenge, but himself cried, 'Friend!'

I write these verses out again because the turning-point that they register seems now, down the perspective of years, even more momentous than I knew it to be when I wrote them.

But – may it not be said? – photographers for the glossy magazines are notoriously more intrusive in Italy than anywhere else. And was it not the post-war Italian cinema that pioneered the keyhole-peeping realism I have objected to? This is true, I think; and although some of those Italian films pleased me, until I was bored by Antonioni and affronted by Visconti, still I know that there is an Italy, of *cinecittà* and the Vittorio Veneto, that would not please me at all if I were pitched into it. My Italy, I am ready to concede and have conceded, is the Italy of the tourist, though of the sort of tourist that Bill Partridge was. This does not mean that it is unpeopled, or that for tourists like us Italian people are only picturesque properties animating the foreground or middle distance of vistas sedulously composed in imagination and memory; I have experienced from them too much civility and consideration for that. One summer after another up to twelve years ago, we returned time and again to the small seaside resort that we lit upon in the first place by accident: Rosignano Solvay, some 30 kilometres south of Livorno. The 'Solvay' half of the name, so unItalian, explains why the foreign visitors stopped a mile short at Castiglioncello or else sped on past, down the howling narrow trench of the Via Aurelia, here squeezed between the railway line and the beaches. For 'Solvay' came from the Belgian-owned chemical factory, which from its tall chimney on the outskirts lazily lofted white and faintly odorous vapours over the modern and humble little town. From the same source, I suppose, came the flat black medallions of sticky naphtha that from time to time spotted the pocked and creviced pumice rocks of the bathing beach. Because of these disadvantages, holiday apartments could be rented cheaply there, and year by year the same two or three Florentine families – women and children, whom the men joined from Florence at weekends – would be found under the same *ombrelloni* leaning from cemented sockets on the pumice. With these families therefore we became familiar, comparing notes annually as their children, of an age with ours, grew into and through adolescence. When my son married, our daughter-in-law declared, half seriously, that being inspected by these Italian friends was more of an ordeal than meeting her husband's kindred.

And of course these Italian families 'lived their life in public'. Seeing and hearing them do so, their vehemence of speech and gesture so much in excess of what by our English standards we thought needful, was part of the pleasure, amused though not condescending, that we took in their company. But is that not at odds with my harping on about privacy? I do not think so. There was nothing immodest about their behaviour. Living life in public, as in the ubiquitous rite of the evening *passeggiata*, had nothing to do with satisfying the watcher through a keyhole. Nothing was stripped, no veils were cast aside. The small dramas that they acted out with such zest were as stylized as grand opera. More intriguingly (to me at any rate), their gesticulations, since they were performed so much in the open as to be seen from anywhere around, seemed sculptural, a series of such gestures as we had seen frozen by Cellini and others in Florence's Piazza della Signoria. Such calculated postures were part of what Stokes taught me to applaud as 'the manifest'; they were thus directly opposite to what might be caught and exposed by a 'candid camera'.

Around me as I write, in a California where the climate but little else is Italian, hang William Partridge's canvases. Only one of them in fact has a Mediterranean subject: the waterfront at Piran, the Italian Pirano, now a Slovenian holiday town where in 1960 (or was it 1962?) we first came together with Bill and his wife Monica. Monica, a Slavic scholar conducting an English-language summer school for the University of Ljubljana, was the reason why any of us were there. And it is on various stony bathing-beaches around Piran that I still see Bill most vividly, his matt-white skin curiously impervious to sunburn; and it is from them, or from above them, that I hear his flat North Midlands accent greeting us with a cordiality that perhaps only I, who grew up with such an accent, could recognize the warmth of.

This little canvas of his, I remember him telling me, was primed very curiously and elaborately indeed, before ever he set paint upon it. A pharmaceutical chemist by trade, Bill had amused himself by reproducing, with his chemist's skills, a way of priming the canvas that he knew of as practised by some Quattrocento painters, long since abandoned by painters in general as too time-consuming and too expensive. And the difference, I persuade myself, shows up: the ground of the painting is so dense that not just the vertical rectangles of the waterfront buildings – white, mauve and ochre – but also the deep blue shading to violet of the sky behind them, and the harbour water in front, start out from the canvas challengingly, implacably, at us, the viewers. The manifest, totally and uncompromisingly itself, not only confronts us, but insists on our taking the force of it. Or so it seems to me, who am no art-critic nor much practised in looking at paintings.

More to the point, I dare say, is the other thing I remember him saying about this painting, where in the foreground the waterfront buildings naturally enough are reflected in the water. Having heard of the technicalities of the priming and so on, one of us ventured to suppose that there was some trick of the trade that he employed to make the colours and even the shapes as reflected, differ from what they reflected. 'No', he returned gently, *'just feeling.'* I was carried then, and am carried now whenever I remember it, not indeed beyond the vocabulary of poetry (for this is Pasternak's vocabulary), but beyond the categories that constrict our responses to poems nowadays. Only today I find someone saying that I have never been able to decide whether, as a poet, I want to be like Doctor Johnson or like Rimbaud. It is such a clever thing to say, and so shallow! I want to be a poet of *feeling*, as Doctor Johnson is, and Rimbaud also.

The point is – or at any rate, *one* point is – that this was said by one who plumes himself on possessing, and by society is rewarded for supposedly having, a special *expertise* precisely about poetry. Because I am a poet who has spent his life in universities, and because I do and always shall attack those who would set the life of poetry against the life of intellect and the life of learning, it is supposed that I do not recognize the blight of academicism. So far am I from any such complacency that I would testify from my own experience how the surest way to reputation as a critic of poetry is to have a firm and profound distrust of what poetry is, and what it does. This is only natural. For the process of *explaining* a poem, as practised by these pundits (I could name names, and they would be distinguished ones), consists precisely in emasculating poetic utterance until it can seem no more than a wayward variant on discursive prose. Since discursive prose is what the English-speaking peoples have agreed to regard as 'understandable', those who reduce to this standard what at first sight transcends it are rightly esteemed and rewarded by the societies for whom they perform this soothing and reassuring service. The worst enemies of poetry are these, its false and sometimes well-meaning friends. And once I had come to see them in this way, I preferred to their company that of painters and sculptors, be they never so ill-informed about literature; as also I preferred to the seminar-rooms of Chicago or Dublin, Cambridge or London, a café-terrace in Cortona or a Californian patio where I could listen to the painter Howard Warshaw or (long ago)

the painter Rico Lebrun. Philip Larkin and Kingsley Amis seem to think
that those who sit late over their wine in Taormina, or Carpinteria in
California, or with Michael Ayrton on a Greek island, are those who sit
similarly late, talking and gesticulating, in Hampstead or Morningside
Heights; it isn't so, and heaven knows how they got to think it was.

That jeer at 'pundits' is a vulgar manoeuvre, and I am ashamed of
myself for stooping to it. But the pundit as I conceive of him commands,
when confronted with literature, a bland composure quite outside the
command of such harried and exacerbated and acrimonious characters as
a Leavis or a Winters. John Bayley and Christopher Ricks are just two of
my contemporaries or near-contemporaries who, though their tone is
more composed, certainly do not figure in my mind as 'pundits'. Another
who doesn't is C. S. Lewis. Lewis, 'Jack' Lewis . . . yes, I knew Lewis, not
well, and not until late; still, I knew him. No quasi-Sicilian, he; but a
hearty Englishman, on the Chesterbelloc model. Or so it was that he
chose to present himself. For he was a great man, but in the English
fashion; that's to say, anxious above all to disguise his greatness out of
some ingratiating and readily available wardrobe – in his case, the port-
flushed Jolly Jack Lewis, good companion of the Combination Room. It
was thus that he 'came on', very dismayingly for me, when he visited
Trinity College Dublin, sometime in the 1950s; and it was in that guise
also that he entertained me, some ten or twelve years later, in Magdalene
College, Cambridge. It was only at the end of that evening, after we had
withdrawn to his rooms from the bonhomie of port and nuts, that he
could bring himself to broach what he felt to be really at issue between us
– my misapprehension, as he thought, of how he felt about the metres
and diction of Sir Thomas Wyatt. However, I have other images of him:
miserably switching one small, stale, burnt-out pipe for another, as he
doggedly sat through, and collaborated in, the marking of examination
papers. For Lewis, sick and ailing as he was, not to be exempted from
such necessary chores was certainly one harshly democratic way for a
society to treat one of its great men.

Lewis of course was genuinely learned, as Leavis and Winters were
not, as certainly I wasn't. He had Greek and Latin and Italian literature at
his finger tips, in a way that has never been possible for me. (For I got a
good education in my 1930s Grammar School, but it wasn't in the least
'classical', despite two years of Greek and five or six years of Latin – hence
my veneration of a great translator like John Dryden, who will convey to
me as much as I shall ever have of what is meant by the Virgilian, the
Ovidian, the Horatian, even the Homeric.) It was the more disconcerting
when, some years later, I read Lewis's admirable romances with one of
my children, to discover that the landscapes of his imagination, as also

those of his Oxonian fellow-anglican J. R. R. Tolkien were insistently *northern*, and seemed not at any point to give access to that mediterranean whose terrain, as mediated by literature, he knew so much better, more exactly and intimately, than I did. I suppose it is not surprising: the Church *of England*, just because it declares itself so proudly 'of England', is perhaps necessarily committed to the landscapes of Northern rather than Southern Europe. But I have sometimes wondered, reflecting for

Family group: 'Gilmerton', Trumpington, 1960

instance on the nonconformist backgrounds of Ruskin and the Brownings, if the non-Anglican is not made free of that mediterranean culture that cradles us all, in a way that most Anglicans cannot be.

This time when I knew Lewis was also the time when we could escape to Italy most often. I was back in Cambridge for my third stint of residence (1958–64). And it was Cambridge that we struggled back to after I had overturned and smashed our car in Friuli on our way back from Piran, and in the process nearly killed my wife. More precisely it was not just Cambridge, but positively Trumpington, that we struggled back to. For our lives had returned us upon ourselves quite uncannily; and we were living only a few hundred yards from the Trumpington general store above which, fifteen years before, we had first set up house. Now we lived on the ground floor of a late-Victorian mansion, since demolished, at the corner of Long Road and Trumpington Road. Perhaps because our landlord, King's College, long ago replaced that house and its neighbour by a block of flats, I remember wistfully its vast and cold and cavernous rooms, the Ruskinian carving on certain banisters, and in particular a mossy lawn under great beech trees. Several of my poems deal directly with that house and that garden; many other poems bring the place back to me, because I remember that I wrote them there, in that ambience of solid amenity, already undermined (for did we not share the house with two other families?), and destined to the demolition-crews as soon as we should have left. That already impending fate, which we were all

Cambridge: Mays Week

aware of, colours the writing that I did there; for those early 1960s still seem to me the years in which modern England was most scandalously disrespectful of the legacies from its past.

My generation came up to University at the time of the Ribbentrop–Molotov pact. Thus there was no excuse for us if we were starry-eyed about the Stalinist Left and, since we weren't, T. S. Eliot's undoubtedly reactionary politics did not disconcert us. What worried and annoyed me, when I returned to Cambridge in 1958, was the way in which the sentimental Left occupied all the same positions, and rehearsed all the same arguments, that I was just old enough to remember from twenty years before. Such manifest inability, on the part of students and their teachers, to learn the plain-as-a-pikestaff lessons of recorded recent history certainly cast a queer and mocking light on the discipline that supposedly we all professed, vowed (so we told ourselves) to 'tradition', to the preserving and handing on of the accumulated and tested experience of previous generations. However, though the positions and the arguments had not changed, the vocabulary had. Where Eliot had been assailed by the Left of the 1930s in overtly political terms, now, in the 1950s, the animus against him was expressed in a more general, an apparently non-political fashion – he seemed not to like *people* very much, in particular he didn't like or celebrate joyous sexuality. It was not hard to see in this the Cambridge Left taking over for its own purposes the vocabulary of a man who was not at all of that way of thinking: Leavis in fact, in his polemics against Eliot on behalf of Lawrence. The duplicity of that manoeuvre offended me. And indeed I seemed to see and hear duplicity everywhere. It was the time when one heard much of 'the people', often dignified – *dignified*, forsooth! – by the epithets, 'ordinary' and 'common'. However, the potent key-word of the 1960s was, I now think, 'class'. From 1959 to 1964, as a Director of Studies at Caius, I exerted myself to recruit young Northerners such as I had been myself twenty years before. But alas, they had all read Richard Hoggart's *Uses of Literacy*; and that division between North and South which I had interpreted as a *cultural* divide, and a challenging one, they interpreted as a *class* distinction, and a non-negotiable one, therefore not challenging in the least. What's more, their 'North' was not metaphorical at all, but literal; and so they wasted the time when they could have been reading, staring into their beer-mugs and accusing themselves of being class-traitors because there they were, in the Little Rose or the Baron of Beef, whereas they ought to have been carousing with the South Shields football team. As year followed year I began to absolve myself from the charge that I had poor judgment when I picked my students, and to think that during my eight years away from England the temper of my nation had drastically changed. What has been called the politics of envy, which I sometimes think of as the politics of self-pity, had sapped independence, self-help and self-respect, and had exalted 'solidarity' – not with the nation of course, but with a section of it – as the highest of all social and political virtues. About this time I began to think that my habits of thought and feeling were so alien to those of my countrymen that my future, if I had one, would have to be spent out of England altogether.

If I ask myself what particular responsibility Cambridge has for this state of affairs, I find myself acquitting my old university with a virtually clear slate. It fought for instance, tenaciously and well, to refuse recognition to the baleful non-science called 'sociology'. What went wrong with its students and its teachers in the 1950s and 1960s was something that was going wrong with the national life in those years, as I discovered to my cost when I left it in 1964 to help found the ill-starred University of Essex. Every instance of elegance or propriety, in the University's social arrangements as in its architecture, was to my Caius undergraduates an affront, since it would be either unnoticed or else misconstrued by a rugby-player from South Shields. Was Trinity College therefore to wear sackcloth and ashes for having been so 'élitist' as to employ, once upon a time, Christopher Wren? The question is absurd; but it is a sort of absurdity that the characteristic polemics of that time pointed towards, and landed themselves in. Because I am myself a man from the West Riding, and count in my family West Riding proletarians as authentic as any that Hoggart takes account of in *The Uses of Literacy*, I feel bitterly that, in that book as in others it has spawned, a real claim that should be made on behalf of such persons has been deflected to serve a rancorous and politically tendentious purpose. The really influential disseminators of this nonsense are not those like Hoggart or Raymond Williams or myself, who know the provincial proletarian and shopkeeper classes from the inside, but the parlour pinks of Hampstead and the Home Counties who, feeling cheated by and guilty about the secure middle-class homes they grew up in, dream up a non-existent alternative, frank and warm, close and earthy, from which they can contrive to feel themselves excluded. Such aberrations were if anything less common in Cambridge than elsewhere in the country, but the fashion for them penetrated the University, and balked the potentialities of more of my pupils than I care to remember.

It was I suppose one day in 1960 or 1961 that, about one o'clock, the 'phone rang in the turreted polygonal room in Caius which I had taken over from Charles Brink. I was just finishing a supervision, and got rid of my pupils in a hurry when the voice on the 'phone identified itself as Kingsley Amis, in Cambridge for the day and asking me to lunch with

Cambridge: 'The turreted polygonal room in Caius'

him. Kingsley was one of several people I had hurried to get acquainted with, some years before, when our names had been linked together by commentators in a literary manifestation of the 1950s which got itself called The Movement – itself, I believe, an important phenomenon for historians of English society and culture, since it represented the first concerted though unplanned invasion of the literary Establishment by the scholarship-boys of the petty bourgeoisie. Kingsley I liked and have always liked, as I like him still; and in fact, if our relations have always been slightly constrained, it's because there is no British writer among my contemporaries whom I have admired more, and the consciousness of that is a little embarrassing to both of us. We lunched together in the University Arms – of all places! (So the old Cambridge hand will exclaim; yet to those who have read Kingsley's novels, it will seem the one right Cambridge locale.) He pumped me about what it was like to teach English in Cambridge, and I was eloquently jaundiced about it, along the lines of my preceding paragraph – only to have to back-pedal, lamely and unconvincingly, when he revealed that that very day he had accepted an invitation from Peterhouse to move there from the post he had held for many years in Swansea. Thus began the brief but eventful and unhappy period when Kingsley was a member of the Cambridge English Faculty. Before long John Holloway and I, who had appeared in anthologies along with Kingsley, had to protest in a faculty meeting when F. R. Leavis, incensed at the Fellows of Peterhouse for making the appointment without consulting the English Faculty, described Kingsley as 'a pornographer'. On the contrary of course he is and always has been a very severe moralist, as one sees from his shocked repudiation of both Philip Roth and Vladimir Nabokov. On the other hand he is a master of comic caprice – a perfectly legitimate and entertaining garment for the moralist to appear in, but one that Cambridge has never been able to account for and acknowledge. Ineffectually wise both before and after the event, I saw the outcome as inevitable. In a justifiably bitter essay that he published afterwards in *Encounter*, Kingsley writes of lunch-time sessions in Miller's Wine Bar in King's Parade; sometimes I was of the company, and enjoyed it.

On another occasion he came to a Caius dinner as Joseph Needham's guest, when my guest was his and my friend Robert Conquest. Also there, I seem to remember, was the Scottish–Polish poet Jimmy Burns Singer who, incurably ill and moving fraily to an untimely death, was to be seen in those years, mostly in Newnham, drinking a quiet and careful pint of beer, a small dog lying at his feet. This memoir would be a more humane document if more of it were taken up with glimpses of such persons, once familiar apparitions in the perspectives of Newnham or

Lyndewode Road or Trinity Street. In such a gallery there would certainly appear, for instance, the stooped figure of H. J. Chaytor, the great scholar of the Romance Languages who was Master of St Catharine's when I went up, who after the war was to be seen in Lyndewode Road or Glisson Road, a shabby shopping bag trailing from his left hand. Is it something about Cambridge, or only something about myself when I am in Cambridge, which brings it about that, whereas my memories of Dublin naturally cluster about particular personalities, my Cambridge memories on the contrary take forms that are unpeopled, polemical and abstract?

One figure at least cannot be allowed to pass from the scene without being established as something more than a peg to hang a polemic upon. This is Douglas, Douglas Brown, who died after a long and crippling illness in 1964. He was out of Cambridge by then, and had been teaching for several years in the English Department at Reading. By then I had long ago grown out of the bemused if also rebellious awe with which I regarded him when he, the brilliantly accomplished and intense Scholar of the college, and I the Exhibitioner, were taught together by Joan Bennett. Over the years I had made as it were a case-study of him, as representing the Cambridge moral ethos in its purity. And though I made my study for compelling and urgent reasons, since I desperately needed to know for the sake of my own identity when to resist that ethos and when to accede to it, nevertheless when Douglas died I had a painful sense, which I have not lost since, of having *used* him and so betrayed him. Douglas himself never made use of men or women in that way, not me nor anyone else, at any rate not consciously. And isn't it just this, in the true-blue Cambridge personality, that makes it so woefully alarmed and at a loss before the comedian, in all the senses of that word? The comedian – whether on the stage or off it, on the television screen or in Miller's Wine Bar – necessarily lives and acts by manipulating his audience, and to that extent *using* it. In that sense Tom Henn, my St Catharine's tutor, was a comedian, as I would guess any Anglo-Irishman has to be. Because of that I imagine that Cambridge was the wrong place for him to be, and that he was not happy through the many decades he spent there, any more than was that comedian of a different stamp, George Rylands. For the purely Cambridge cast of mind, if I knew it (as I think I did) in Douglas, does not know what to make of any striking of attitudes, any provisional trying-out of postures towards experience, any donning or doffing of alternative masks, any switchings of viewpoint, except as insincerity, lack of seriousness. To this Cambridge mind, with its blade-like directness, any of these more or less histrionic manoeuvrings before experience is profoundly distasteful. And yet to personalities of another cast, just these obliquities of provisional assent are the natural ways by which to arrive, in all

137

seriousness, at sincerity, identity, truthfulness. Douglas was gentle and self-critical, and he would have readily enough agreed with this last contention; and yet his temperament was such that, though he would have given conscious assent, his heart would not have been in it. And thus, though he recognized my badinage when I plied him with it – even, I think, he quite liked the feel of it – of affecting images which rise to my memory when I think of him, not one presents him as laughing, even less than heartily. He was in earnest, always; he could not help it, that was his nature. He had a sense of humour, right enough; but he did not like it, nor trust it – it seemed irreverent, as of course it is.

Douglas in his last weeks in the Reading hospital, when drugs had mercifully clouded his judgment, talked of recovering enough to pay his first visit to Italy, if we would attend him. Of course I said we would. But how would it have been, if we had gone there? I just don't see him in that ambience, or against any of those backgrounds. Better for him, I think, Switzerland or Germany – realms of sublimity and of the sublime music that, like the true puritan he was, he responded to with an intensity that was almost shocking. (Or so I found it, I, who have always thought of music, whether 'sublime' or popular, that I could take it or leave it – and mostly I have left it.) And since Cambridge for me was and is embodied in Douglas Brown, I have never been able to feel a relation between Cambridge and the Mediterranean. This is perverse. Do not Wren's Trinity Library and James Gibbs's Senate House triumphantly vindicate their implied claim that Mediterranean idioms can be acclimatized in the clammy and fog-wreathed fens? I can only say that that isn't how I experience them. These buildings are beautiful, certainly; and with Wren's Library I can define the beauty more exactly – as an emphatic and masculine declaration in stone. And yet there is something glacial about them, as about the landscape-architecture that created the Cambridge backs as a whole. Magnificent, these assertions in the teeth of the Siberian wind! And I know a mood in which I cherish most, of all artistic statements, these that are made in despite and in defiance of climate and terrain. Yet in another frame of mind, one that on the whole I trust further, I find myself thinking that the most robust and virile art is uttered not so as to contradict its natural ambience, but on the contrary so as to articulate it, bring it to a point.

These are fine-drawn speculations. I can bring them down to earth by reporting that Doreen and I, like many others before us, found the Cambridgeshire landscape quite lugubriously *flat*. Since she was of the West Country, and I was of the North, and since the Italy that we first made our own was hilly Tuscany, there is perhaps little wonder that we

found Gibbs's Senate House or his building in King's, though undoubtedly splendid, oddly unanchored in the earth that they rose from, or
were imposed upon. Our spirits rose whenever, westward, we climbed
Madingley Hill, or, south-eastward, we approached Saffron Walden
and the land began to slope and swell.

At any rate, the poems that I wrote from or about Italy in these years
characteristically defined that Italy by contrast with the East Anglian
England that we had departed from and returned to. One of these poems
is called 'Hornet':

> In lilac trained on the colonnade's archway, what
> Must be a hornet volleys lethally back
> And forth in the air, on the still not hot
> But blindingly white Italian stone, blue-black.
>
> I have seldom seen them in England, although once
> Years ago the foul-mouthed, obligingly bowed
> Rat-catcher of Cambridge made a just pretence
> To a cup of tea, for a nest cleared in the road.
>
> Those were wasp-coloured, surely; and this blue,
> Gun-metal blue, blue-black ominous ranger
> Of Italy's air means an Italy stone all through,
> Where every herb of holier thought's a stranger.
>
> No call for such rage in our England of pierced shadows.
> Stone's and the white sun's opposite, furious fly,
> There no sun strides in a rapid creak of cicadas
> And the green mould stains before the mortar is dry.

I think that holds the balance even. No one who knows that I was
Douglas's friend, that already as a schoolboy I knew I was a countryman
of Richard Rolle of Hampole, could suppose that 'herb of holier thought'
is written lightly or scornfully. And in the end, I have no doubt, the
pierced shadows of England – initially observed, I remember, in the
garden of our Trumpington house, 'Gilmerton' – command my allegiance
more than the more dramatic Italian confrontation of light with shade. Yet
those ambiguous hues, those betwixt-and-between apparitions of the
English climate, have, I sometimes think, a deleterious effect on the
intellectual life of England, at least in fields which are of the first impor-
tance to me. Where else but in England, I ask myself, does a clear-cut
disagreement about a professional matter, for instance about the proper
diction for poetry, get itself so immediately cross-hatched with shadows
thrown from irrelevancies like egalitarian humanism or wounded *amour-
propre*? The fly, furiously stung and stinging with an appetite for consum-
mate orderings, has a right to his furies; but he buzzes awry and at

Cambridge: 'crepuscular, approximate . . . fugitive or hulking shadows'

random, bewildered among more or less creditable approximations, pierced shadows, neither true light nor true dark.

And thus the rigour on which Cambridge so plumes itself quite signally fails to operate in the area that for me will always matter more than any other – the realm of artistic performance. F. R. Leavis spent himself through a lifetime, hectoring Cambridge with his message that there are questions to which the answer is 'Yes' or 'No', not 'Yes, perhaps' or 'No, unless . . .' But now as when Leavis began, the poems that come out of Cambridge are just what they always were: at best sensitive, intelligent, well-mannered, but never conclusively and passionately *clinched*. I am prepared to believe, now, that this is inevitable. It is a matter of light, and the climate. As the fog swirls into Trinity Street in the early afternoon, or hangs there until nearly midday, as the warm lights high in the walls wink on and glow through the haze, I recognize the irremediably Gothic Cambridge that I best know and love. And how can the art that comes of such weather be anything but crepuscular, approximate, a composition of fugitive or hulking shadows?

10

Americans

Pierre Boulle, in his thriller of 1965, *Garden on the Moon*, has two German *émigrés*, rocket-scientists, confide to each other how they feel about the Americans they are working for, and the American nation they have joined:

> '. . . I had to put real pressure on them to get them to make a thorough check of every missile. Otherwise they would have launched the whole lot in a couple of weeks, out of sheer curiosity, from love of experimenting just for the sake of experimenting, without being discouraged by the failures, feeling convinced that each of these taught them something . . . which was true, of course.'

> 'They always think first and foremost of experimenting,' Meyer muttered.

> 'Afterward, on the other hand, they work like beavers to try to find the reason for the failure. They love *feeling their way*. We feel our way when we can't do otherwise. With them it's for pleasure. And it's the same in every field . . .'

In another writer, particularly if he were British, the point of this exchange would be to jeer at the Germans for being, *having to be*, so doggedly methodical. But that seems not to be Pierre Boulle's intention. And when I read, 'it's the same in every field', I am made to think. However it may be with those metal and electrical contraptions that are rocket-propelled to the moon and beyond, certainly those verbal contraptions that have most interested me do show, when fabricated by Americans, the features that Boulle's characters talk about. One such contraption, Ezra Pound's *Cantos*, has over many years fascinated and exasperated me in a way that I cannot account for. Other such contraptions – Louis Zukofsky's *A.*, *Paterson* by William Carlos Williams, Charles Olson's *Maximus Poems* – have interested me less, and in some cases not at all. (*Paterson* I have never had time for.) But all of them, I see, do have the characteristics that Pierre Boulle's fictitious Germans try to isolate: 'experimenting just for the sake of experimenting', indifference to 'failures', love of 'feeling their way'.

The Englishman is in two minds about this. On the one hand, 'feeling their way' looks like a version of that procedure so beloved of the English empiricist, his 'muddling through'; on the other hand these American poems, of which the earliest example no doubt is Walt Whitman's 'Song of Myself', are for most English readers *unreadable*, in the thoroughly legitimate sense that, even if the reader is earnest and assiduous, still 'life is too short'. There is too, in the Englishman's sense of the matter, something comical about the simply measurable *enormity* of these undertakings. And then there is, for good or ill, the Englishman's distrust of the theoretical. For American poets like Pound or Olson, though they 'feel their way', nevertheless theorize about it, both before and during the event. One way to solve the dilemma, a way that appeals to me, is to maintain that, however it may be in other areas, 'muddling through' has never been the procedure of the English artist, who has been on the contrary – think of George Herbert and Robert Herrick – characteristically a precisian, and a miniaturist. Another way of saying this would be that in all the arts the English way has been towards blurring the distinction between artist and craftsman.

At any rate – and odd as I now find it in retrospect – the occasion that I found for exercising my English sensibility in these American structures was in Pierre Boulle's country; specifically, in Touraine.

The years were 1972 and 1973; when we lived, much of the time, in a rented 'particulier' in Tours, in rue Jolivet. It all should have happened long before, since French is the only foreign language that I can speak and read with confidence and tolerable correctness; it was the merest chance that postponed my French experiences until so late. Several poems came out of it – notably, one of thanks to old Fiery Evans of Barnsley Grammar School, who inculcated the language that gave me access to the lives and landscapes I moved among; and another longer piece in several sections called 'In the Stopping Train', which originated in a miserable journey by rail from Tours to Paris and back, through heavy rain much of the time, on a fruitless attempt to keep a rendezvous with the Irish poet John Montague. But the fullest rendering of all that French experience, and the most heartfelt expression of my excited gratitude for it, is a poem that I must probably learn to think of as a folly of my middle age. I have never published it except in a truncated form in a magazine. It has at least the interest of a curiosity; being the response to France of an Englishman who seems to be trying, because of the form he has adopted, to think and feel like an American. Those British readers who are averse to American poetry, or to any poetry which acknowledges that Ezra Pound has composed or perpetrated his *Cantos*, had better skip the next several pages, on which this poem appears. American readers on the other hand will not, I hope, unanimously exclaim: 'Would that he had written thus always!'

Enough! The thing may or may not be an abortion; let me at least be delivered of it, with not much more by way of preface. But with this much more: first, because the response behind the poem was heartfelt, the

143

experience which it records has to hook on to my experiences up to that point – in a word, on to my Englishness; and secondly, it is meant to matter that the poem, in this its final version, is named for a French naval hero, Aristide du Petit-Thouars, whose family home, Bournois, can still be visited, there in Touraine. So far as I can understand my own motives, this puts the piece along with others that I have written about naval heroes, British ones like James Trevenen and Vancouver and Cochrane, and one Irish-American, Commodore John Barry. Shades of Henry Newbolt's 'Drake's Drum', and poems by a nowadays shabbier figure, Alfred Noyes! I do not disdain the company. Indeed with poor old Noyes, slack writer though he is, I feel some kinship. For he was another English writer who lived in California – in Santa Barbara, I think – and wrote about it. And this may be much to the point; for what Trevenen and Vancouver and Cochrane had in common was that they were all active on the Pacific coast of the Americas, and it seems to me I was intrigued by the thought of their British sensibilities, like mine so long after, trying to engage with landscapes so remote not just in space, but in scale and in history, from the English experience. That is probably a too schematic explanation why through several years after 1968 these men, and other explorers and navigators along that coast – for instance, the compatriot of Petit-Thouars, La Pérouse – should have excited my imagination as they did. I dare say that in the outcome, as I went into these lives more deeply, the motive became simpler and bolder, and more like Henry Newbolt's: nothing less than the heroic, the humanly heroic as inscribed less on history (where it always turns out to be ambiguous, as Cochrane's did) than on charts and maps, on geography. None of this, except simply the fact of heroism, bears on the case of Petit-Thouars, of whom in any case I know only what I learned from two sentences in the *Guide Michelin*. But it was certainly in the back of my mind as I wrote the poem, which accordingly in this tenuous way hooks on to the California I had come from and would return to, as well as on to the England of Turpin's Lane – that England whence my father had in his time also gone to France, to the trenches of Picardy and Flanders.

PETIT-THOUARS
(Guide Michelin)

The reticule is infinite, anything
is in this bag;
        as see (he quotes
himself), 'in an Armstrong-
      Siddeley tourer,
        percheron of the twenties,'

famous horse of
    le Perche-Gouët:
à robe gris pommelé
noir, ou abère
(red-roan)
and predominantly
    of Arab blood.   Guillaume
              Gouët possessed
in the eleventh
    century 5
    baronies, of which
Brou la Noble, a waystage
            Chartres to
    St. Jacques de Compostelle; and
MONTMIRAIL LA SUPERBE
    un décor Louis Quinze
    de la princesse de Conti.

                This
reticule is capacious: horses
go into it, shaggy hooves thrashing
through cisMississippian forests
paw at a stand
(said Walter Prescott Webb)
    before the great *puszta* of Texas.

Well, how it weaves, how it nets
    the wind, this energy
    in solitude!
            These armchair
energies unpick
    the pricking steeds
    of Spenser!   Tapestries
picked, unpicked; unwound
and wound again.   Who knows
           how it is grounded, how
tell the unsound from the solid
machicoulis that crown
Chateau St. Jean
in Nogent-le-Rotrou?

And he does not need even to go there!
    yet will, he will discover
minuscule village perdu
dans ses collines, its low
        pavillons locked through the year
        against a Parisian's summer:
self-cancelling perditions.

Will go!   the exit
    from *voyages autour de sa chambre;*
    an act of will, an act of

faith in there being somewhere
a place where the wind blows in,
    a breach, a gaping
    way from *le Perche-Gouët*
into his chamber, into the chambering
locks and lewdness of MIND.

Also his 'she',
she has to be reassured
somewhere there is
a paddock full of those noble
astonishingly low-slung horses
at Brou la Noble perhaps,
at Montmirail la Superbe,
          Yarrows unvisited.

A SHE like Rider Haggard's
not less exacting:
             'Show me
la fontaine Bellerie,
not a municipal wash-place!'
    The master-poet's friend,
Belleau the *nogentais*
the French Anacreon,
    practised an ancient ease
    diseased and exiled. Did he
prattle to some purpose?
    Oh my 'she', my 'she',
        what purpose pacifies
        you, or that part of me
        that I have, loving you?
You do not care for horses.
Olson came to our house
once, and he is as dead
now as Rémy Belleau.

Reticulations, *dis*
séminations, dis
placements. *Guide Michelin*
to gloomy Dis.

Hot silence under the clock
at Montmirail where I hide
behind dark glasses, heavy-
jowled in the hired car's mirror.
    And Montmirail is less
    superb, though there the rash
    Plantagenet fledged his four
    eagles, than on a haywain
    Thyrsis astraddle, hayfork
    straight rule across his hams;
in snowy singlet and hat

146

against the sky on a haycart,
hayfork a solid rule.
    That was among the red
    weals of the poppies and
    the long roads straight and empty,
    the slender skittles of poplars.
And here at the end in the hot
steep silence of Montmirail
a grocer tells me of four
Percheron mares still working
a farm outside Le Mans.

    Or as my master has it:
    'never an ape or a bear' –
            Ezra Pound in his youth
            walking the roads of France,
            hearing of gypsies, horses,
            menageries, always the other
            side of the hill, of the forest . . .

Well, but I found them, forests;
after a cold beer, found them,
more scents than ferny Hewlett
dreamed of, the roads so dappled,
    though not Bournois, although
    caché dans les arbres
    ce château.

    Down Turpin's Lane at nightfall
        diminishing vista;
    under the overhanging
    boughs, a dwindling shape
    runs ahead alone,
    a child, my own; and the pipe,
    reed, hazel, or oat,
    lifts its menacing minors.

    A figure has leapt the hedge
    out of the wheat, and it stands
    unnaturally still
    slouch-hatted hard by the oak
    disposing scythe and hone.

Tapestry-panel!

    picked, unpicked,/   the hangings
    of how much more than *ma chambre*?

How much more?

    In *La Beauce*
    (puszta) the tractors crawl
    where once the percherons
        the so much more

147

alien corn still falls
behind them, under the small
    viaduct of
        a monorail
unfinished, and the finished
acres inch year by year
out under billboards and pylons.

'Your lordship has forgotten me . . .
We met at Clarendon . . . and last
at Montmirail in Maine.'
To Eliot's Becket, his
ghostly accuser.
        They
are around us, our accusers,
This is one purpose must
pacify.
      (Does it?)
         We must
be glad of them
standing in wait at nightfall
    on our account and our children's,
thronged oblivion standing
around us, edging under
    splotches of shade.   Mad Clare,
Thyrsis angles the whetted
    edge that accuses bone.

Not all perditions are
self-cancelling, the *bocage*
is sometimes uncannily still.
Even outside the joke
city of Frinton-on-Sea,
oaks creak at nightfall over
the hedgehog gouged by a blade
uncannily handled, un-
musically.   And
    as for a meeting-place of druids,
    on motor-assisted bicycles the locals
    zing in the *bois sacré*.
A loneliness inviolate of course
           can be *distrait*,
    and we are panicked, we are so ashamed,
    the hedge of brush is tense with irritation.

Inviolate, however violated
– it is ourselves we ravage, not the shades –
is how to think of sacrificial groves,
mournfully; and as
glades persisting through
    a forest felled
is how to think of lanes

like Turpin's, where it takes
two twists off into hush
and the sound dies of the vans
passing along to Frinton.

Closing in is an opening
out here as between
    sheaved sprays
black-green, minutely heaving
in the last of the July light it
                not reassuringly
beckons.
    Yes!   it will have,
imperiously it wants,
something
of us.
    A chink
among many, among slashes,
splotches, medals of pale
light, the chink of metal
against the light has come with
verdigris' discolored
aura: the gone team's headbrass,
there where it flashed on the turn
of 1915, is
looped up ahead in a crotch
of unlocatable timber!

The long kind slope and profile of
Dobbin, old Dad
the headbrass on it jouncing as it
moves.   It has got to move.   We
will go, will to go, not any
more, not backwards, not that yearning, not the
guidebook *again*! The Old Realm has to, if
perditions self-destruct and after
however long a circuit
of crooning history, cancel out those
honeyheads of Rat's Park, every
gradual dusk a drawing down of
blinds, it has to,
however stone-struck, stunned
museum-piece, however
its guts festoon and foil it, heave itself
up, however bloodied, it must come
now, one step, one stumbling step, towards us.

Rat's Park: he runs
ahead alone
from the appalling latrine,
           and the scyther

sniper speaks.   He goes down
my own.   He squeals
like a hedgehog, kneecap smashed.

At 40 he learned to ride.
My learning is in
                  the wards of Mind.
At 52 I force
a lock that has not turned
in 60 years

* *

Not that it matters.   In a dark
wood, not really.   Forest felled, I fly
adown the glade, down the long glad of it
like my own child.   If child of God, then how
so self-observed? I father myself, I walk
staidly along behind myself; not really
much of a worry any more, this being
my own familiar.   Abba, I make bold to
say My Father all too bold.   Say Our
Father, oh yes but saying My
Father, it's all too much. I move as a wraith
of memory, father and son, in my duplicity
down Memory Lane called Turpin's.   Who
fathers such a double phantom?   Squeal,
if I could squeal would be much, as when
19 years back for a lost child imagined raped
I jabbered through the eucalyptus grove
off the end of Bluff Drive, nerves
jabbering obscenities. Our ageing
evacuates all senses, not just five.   For children
lost, grown up, what care I if the scyther
speaks?   Not nothing.   But just what,
how, and how much?   A long way past the *mezzo*
del cammin, North Sea at most a mile off.

And screens of trees so scanty, so transpierced!
I need the dark wood darker.   Groundless swell,
well-being floats us with such levity
down Turpin's Lane at twilight.   Best, the child
discerned through a following father's eyes – the father
levitated, more than a little 'high' –
best, blest the babe, bowled down the darkening alley
precipitate of what desired conjunction
in what retort, what loins?   Metallurgy!
Except the thing is malleable, is ductile
past our conceiving of it.   No
matter but metamorphosis.
Is such a world worth writing for or about?
Sing it on tapes if you like, but I will not
inscribe (subscribe) it here.

150

Il y a des choses, there are some things
beyond this fiddle, though
the sense of an ending, the sense of 'presentness', even
the sense of 'horse' are
significantly different/
      in French and English – wherefore
these in themselves absurd
divagations in French. That *pavillon*
should mean among other things 'colours',
the sort one strikes, as in
striking camp? (Goodbye,
little house, for another year)
      does seem
something more than striking/
       intriguing. One
strikes or refuses to strike, one is
or is not Aristide
du Petit-Thouars, who was

560 to 468
B.C., one of the ten
at Marathon, called THE JUST

and gloriously fell
at Aboukir, upon
his quarter-deck, would not
(Petit-Thouars) abide
amener son pavillon.

  Now that I have copied out the poem 'Petit-Thouars', I discover that I'm
not ashamed of it. And yet, does it earn its place in this book? For who in
France were my companions? One to be sure was the woman who
demanded to see Ronsard's *fontaine Bellerie*; another was the young
man, who, then a child, had bounded away before me down Turpin's
Lane; another was the young woman whom, years before when she
was a child, I had sought with frantic obscenities through a Californian
eucalyptus-grove. But these – my wife, my daughter, one or other or both
of my sons – have been present, without my needing to say so, through
many earlier chapters. Their various presences could be, or at least they
have been, taken for granted – which does not mean that I am not grateful
to them. From this poem however, it would appear that whereas in Italy I
had the company (more often in imagination than in fact) of Bill Partridge,
in France my only companions were the members of my immediate
family. In fact this is not the case, it is the poem I wrote that makes it seem
so. And this is because it is written on a different plan from my other
poems. Its plan is egocentric; it assumes, or it must seem to assume,
that the geographical and historical entity called France has no value,

perhaps no significant existence, outside what it does to one sensibility, my own. This has always seemed to me overweening, and poetry written on that plan to be in that way childish, screaming, 'Me! Me!' One remembers: 'Song of Myself'. As Louis Simpson has said, such poems are really do-it-yourself kits. That cannot be right; yet where do we find a secure standpoint from which to write poems on another plan, by which Frenchmen called Petit-Thouars and Belleau, and innumerably unnamed Frenchmen and Frenchwomen of their days and of our own, would be acknowledged to have existed independently, at times when the poet was not there to observe them, or think about them? Throughout my working lifetime everything has favoured poetry written on the other plan. Egocentric is what poetry has been thought to be, necessarily, as it were by definition; and poetry which is not thus egocentric has been held to be not poetry at all, or poetry only by courtesy, of a second or third order of intensity. I have thought this wrong, and I think so still; and rightly or wrongly I think of it as a characteristically American error.

And yet . . . there are Americans, and Americans. These Americans of the Atlantic coast – Whitman and Pound, Zukofsky and Williams and Olson – are looking always to Europe, even if they look there (as Williams did) only to repudiate furiously most of what they see. There is quite another America, invoked by my diary for August 1958: '5 p.m., depart Salt Lake City (car D.6); 8 a.m., arrive Denver; 12.15, depart Denver (car 89);

Grinnell, Iowa, 1958: Curtis Bradford (right) with one of his sons and D.D.

2.33 a.m. arrive Grinnell.' Grinnell, Iowa – the heartland! No state in the Union gets sneered at so often as Iowa, alike by East-coast Americans and by Americans of the other, the Pacific coast, confronting the Orient as Whitman and Pound confronted Europe. (For that is yet another 'America', as I have allowed for by writing a chapter called 'Californians'.) What it would be like to spend a lifetime in Grinnell, Iowa, I cannot imagine; though sometimes I think that, despite the ice-storms of the long winter and the tornados of the hot and humid summer, it might be a sort of slumbrous idyll – too slumbrous, indeed, for my liking. What is certain is that no one knows America who does not know, from living there, Iowa or its neighbouring states – Missouri perhaps, Wisconsin, or Nebraska. Living so far from any or either ocean – one has to have done it, to know what it is like. The gibe is that those who best know that life flee from it as soon as they can; and hence that native Iowans figure for instance largely in the census returns for greater Los Angeles. But that may prove only that Los Angeles and Hollywood, having built an industry out of catering to the fantasies of the shallowest and least sturdy Americans, have succeeded all too well in attracting to themselves the most foolish and childish citizens of other states. The Midwest is what we are talking of: and its laureates for me have been Hamlin Garland, in short stories set in Iowa and Wisconsin, the extraordinary solitary poetess of Wisconsin, Lorine Neidecker, and Willa Cather in that Nebraskan classic, *My Antonia*. Most Americans who have come from one or the other coast to this mid-America have shuddered and retreated as fast as they could; but a few, the strongest and most sensitive, have stayed in those parts long enough to find there a poetry stranger, and more definitively American, than they could find on either coast. It is a poetry – for instance, Lorine Neidecker's – not of experimental 'contraptions'. Though the end-product may look like that (Neidecker's for instance looking like Zukofsky's or George Oppen's), it has been arrived at by processes quite different and more innocent, simply by trying to come to terms with spaces so vast and weather so extreme, with the help of a history so scanty. It is not my sort of poetry – on the contrary, it frightens and repels me; but just because it is so alien, I know it to be authentic.

At any rate, there we were – my twelve-year-old son and I – descending in the humming early hours from the Rock Island 'Rocket', to be met, there at Grinnell's little 'depot', by Curtis Bradford, wheeling his push-bike. And with him, with Curtis, we walked perhaps half a mile to his frame-house in the elm-shaded Main Street where, as I write, Curtis's widow Maria still lives. I have been told that the Grinnell depot – a 'halt' we would call it, in British usage – has been long abandoned, though two crazy rocking-chairs still stand on the platform where, as late as our second visit in 1965, one could still mount or descend from trains to Chicago, to Omaha and Denver.

The bicycle was Curtis's vehicle. It was one of his eccentricities, and a most unlikely one in an American of his generation, that he had never learned to drive a car. How this happened, or could have happened, in a country so dependent on the automobile as Curtis's America, is something I cannot explain. It made him – even in Grinnell, where everything was in walking or cycling distance – dependent on the good offices of others, and particularly dependent on Maria, a small brown athletic whipcord of a woman, with her heavy German accent and prematurely white hair. But 'dependence' was not how Curtis made it appear when he pressed into service as chauffeur Maria or anyone else – even, on occasion, me. Quite the contrary! The mechanics of mere driving, he made one feel, was a menial concern below the notice of such a natural aristocrat as himself. Particularly was this the case when in January 1965 he met us at the airport in Des Moines, after we had flown from Connecticut by way of Chicago. He was attended by a younger colleague, who then drove us all to Grinnell in bitter sub-zero weather over icy and snowy roads at which I blanched. But Curtis was every inch the *grand seigneur*,

Winter's end in Midwest: 'In a white world there are so many kinds of white'

from the moment when, in elegantly slanted soft hat and ulster worn like a cape, he greeted us at the airport. Never a thought did he give, apparently, to the hazards so magnanimously, and it must be said confidently, navigated by Jim Kissane.

This indeed was another of the surprisingly many things about Curtis that I did not understand, and cannot explain: where did it come from, this good opinion that he had of himself? I thought once that it was all in the name, that he must be of a Mayflower family, descended from Governor Bradford of the Plymouth colony; and yet I believe, when I enquired, I found that wasn't the case – the family was an old one, but not so old as that. Could it be defensive over-compensation for teaching in a college so small and out-of-the-way as Grinnell? Hardly; for, small though it is, Grinnell is very much an élite institution with, among the knowledgeable, a deservedly high reputation as a liberal arts college like Oberlin or Bowdoin. Small it is, however; and Curtis, a publishing scholar in a predominantly teaching institution, had for many years been a big fish in what could not help but be a little pool. I dare say that explanation comes nearer the mark. But it doesn't satisfy me, and I don't want it to. For I see Curtis as representative; representing an American type which, though rarer than it used to be, can still be met with – the sort of American who, knowledgeable about the Old World, is sure that his New World has surpassed it – not just politically and industrially, but culturally too. I don't remember that Curtis and I ever spoke of American domestic politics. And that vexes me; for he must surely have held that *his* New World was not the world of the demagogue, who had long before come to dominate United States politics even more markedly than the politics of Europe. Curtis must have been élitist, surely, in a way that American politics in his day, and for long before, made no provision for. And yet I cannot be sure: slender, elegant, always looking younger than his years, Curtis I suspect was so imperturbably sure of the superiority of American character and American society that he might well have admitted the existence of demagoguery in the United States, yet remained sure that his nation could contain and control it as the older nations had not. Accordingly, being Curtis's friend, and staying his friend, was not easy, if one was non-American; when he was at his most affable, still a hint of condescension hung in the air, and when he was not affable (as in 1965 he rather often wasn't) the animosity was more than hinted at. This was not pleasant; and we would not have put up with it, if we had not known that by then he was sick, and drinking too much, if we had not been in sort his guests, and if we had not remembered earlier occasions when he had been 'in better shape'.

We had known him first in the 1950s, in Dublin, when he and Maria and their four children had installed themselves in a suburban house in Rathfarnham, so that Curtis could get access, through Mrs Yeats, then still living in Palmerston Road, to those manuscripts and work-sheets of Yeats which, when subsequently published, earned Curtis his solid though belated scholarly reputation. In those days, as memory brings them back to me, he was not a difficult companion. And he paid us the great compliment, when the time came for the Bradfords to entertain Mrs Yeats, of asking Doreen and me to make up the company. To be sure, the invitation had a twist to it; if we were able to come, and since Curtis did not drive, could he prevail on us to pick up Mrs Yeats and drive her out to Rathfarnham? After all, Palmerston Road was on the way. So it was; and so we did. It was, I vividly remember, a bitter and icy evening, uncommon in Dublin. Snag-toothed George Yeats was after all an Englishwoman, with a liking for mischief and all her wits about her for as long as I knew her. So I sometimes wonder if Curtis's offensiveness about the British, fifteen years later, was not paying off a score which Mrs Yeats and I had run up against him that evening. For, with how much conscious malice I do not now remember, but certainly with some, I turned the conversation after dinner from Yeats to his friend Ezra Pound, the author of *Hugh Selwyn Mauberley* – author of other works also, but at that time *Mauberley* was the only one I felt secure about. Curtis was quite unprepared, in a way that must now seem strange. A respectable 'Yeatsian' nowadays would know that he had somehow to come to terms with the figure of Pound, and the significance of the long and intimate relation between the two poets. But this was the early 1950s, when the pioneer in understanding Pound, Hugh Kenner, had not yet broken the ground for the rest of us; when, accordingly, it was still possible for admirers of Yeats, as of T. S. Eliot also, to regard Pound as an outlandish and unreliable adventurer whose association with either of the two admirable poets was an unfortunate accident, unscrupulously engineered by Pound himself to be an embarrassment (though not a serious one) to both Yeats and Eliot, and to Yeats's and Eliot's readers. Whether Pound had or had not (opinions differed) in his youth achieved some writing of slender distinction, the adjacent presences of Yeats and Eliot having presumably made that possible, Pound's subsequent career – whether in poetry (the *Cantos*), or in politics (his espousal of Fascist Italy) – was self-evidently disgraceful, sterile and yet dangerous. Had he not lately escaped a charge of treason by pleading, or having it pleaded for him, that he was, and had been for some years, insane? And accordingly was he not at that very moment compassionately held, by the direction of the United States government, in a hospital for the insane in Washington? Something like that, if memory serves, was what Curtis came up with, in a tone distinctly nettled and far from compassionate. At which point Mrs Yeats weighed in. Pound was mad? Well but of course 'Ezra' was mad, always had been. And she recalled him living in Kensington, firing off letters to the rector of the nearby church, protesting at 'the confounded bells', and how they disturbed his concentration. It became apparent that in George Yeats's vocabulary 'mad' was a word to be used affectionately and indulgently, as when one says of a greatly relished friend, 'Oh, he's crazy.' And as for Pound's influence on Yeats, 'Ezra', she declared flatly, 'was always right about W. B. – *always*!' Consternation! Curtis could not have been much more disconcerted that I was, who had provoked more mischief than I knew how to deal with. How the tatters of the evening were patched together, I do not now remember, though I have the impression that Mrs Yeats remained unperturbed. Indeed I now suspect that she was making a monkey out of both and all of us. For as we drove her home she remarked: 'People say Ezra's Cantos are difficult. *I* don't find them difficult, do *you*?' I like to believe that my reply was lost in the noise of my changing gear.

Willowy Curtis Bradford! Why did he so often abash me in life? And why is it that even now, when I summon from the past his clean-shaven face that only at close quarters seemed to have profited from the deftest plastic surgery, still he is able to put me out of countenance? On the one hand I seem to take him as the accredited spokesman of that mid-America which, just because it is so far from the Atlantic seaboard, can afford to take only a tepid and remote interest in my Englishness, and to bend a cold and sceptical eye on British pretensions generally. And indeed his mordancy about the poor showing of British literary scholarship since 1945 is a true bill, as was his indictment of the patent anti-Americanism in too many of the anonymous reviews in *The Times Literary Supplement* of those years. And yet Curtis was a Midwesterner only by adoption; it was a New Englander in voluntary exile who imported Moselle wines through special arrangements with a shipper in Chicago, and would un-cork and taste them in the heat of an Iowan summer evening, with a formality to which I felt as inadequate as did his half-grown uneasy sons. How much of that too was a skilfully projected illusion? Perhaps he was no more a connoisseur than I was. If so, the illusion was magisterially sustained; as it was when I drove him, staying with us in Trumpington in 1960, on an excursion to Woburn Abbey, and felt like apologizing for it, so vulgar a house as it seemed, both inside and out. It must indeed have been the New Englander in Curtis – more particularly, the graduate of either Harvard or Yale (Yale, I believe) – who worked this disabling spell. For I have felt the same charm cast by others, American expatriates in expensive restaurants in Italy and France, moving there with an enviable

The Ashley river, South Carolina: 'yet another America, and the one most haughtily aware of its distinctiveness'

ease, and a command both of languages and social rituals, such as made me feel clumsy and provincial by contrast. Scott Fitzgerald's Dick Diver must surely have been a Princeton man; but it is the early chapters of *Tender is the Night* which best convey, in Dick Diver and the circle he draws about him, the charmed and charming life which one sort of American used to lead, and perhaps still leads, in Europe. Such Americans – one thinks of Logan Pearsall Smith and Bernard Berenson, though neither is a representative case – in their way were better Europeans, more knowledgeable and at ease, than ever any European was. Of this sort of Europeanized American, the Southerner Allen Tate (voice of yet another America, and the one most haughtily aware of its distinctiveness) wrote waspishly and yet with some justice:

> The homes and the universities of New England became a European museum, stuffed with the dead symbols of what the New Englander could not create because provision for it had been left out of his original foundation. In the nineteenth century New England confessed her loss of the past by being too much interested in Europe.

In Curtis perhaps, because I seem not to have pressed him on this issue any more than on others, I encountered only the illusion of this expertise, not the fact of it. But I have met other Americans – New Yorkers as well as New Englanders – who have daunted me by their lightly worn knowledgeability about Europe, and indeed specifically about England. Is it only a craven defensiveness that makes me concur with Allen Tate in finding, in that familiarity of theirs, something glacial and sterilizing?

At any rate, how many Americas, and how many kinds of American, I have known! Enough to make me sure that there are at least as many that I have so far had no chance to know. And enough to make me exasperated and dumbfounded at the glibness with which generalizations about America and Americans are bandied about among the English, including many who ought to know better. Not twenty years ago, in Cambridge, I was party to a conversation between F. R. Leavis and C. S. Lewis, illustrious antagonists on many famous issues and occasions, who agreed however that there could not be in any serious sense universities on American soil because – and I don't remember which of the revered elders triumphantly produced this moth-eaten proposition – the United States was not a democracy but (wait for it!) a plutocracy. Sagely nodding and capping each other's observations, Lewis and Leavis would hear nothing of expostulations from me, or from another of the company lately returned from a year in the States. I fear that even today, among English people not much less distinguished, one can hear the same irresponsible assurance about an America which they have never taken the trouble to

159

inspect at all extensively or closely. In most cases, I suspect, the root cause of this is an angry and unsure defensiveness about England, a sentiment which some of these people have the nerve to present as patriotic. At any rate, having known so many anti-American Englishmen, I deserved to meet, in Curtis, an anglophobe American.

From my boyhood, when no American was to be expected in the streets of Barnsley, I recall mistily a stereotype of which the origin may lie, like so much else in English mythology of that day and since, in the books of P. G. Wodehouse: the American, we somehow gathered, looked rather like the delightful film-comedian, Harold Lloyd – he wore horn-rimmed spectacles and loud checks, he was larger than most of us, or else he seemed so because of a large and expansive (that is to say, insensitive) manner. Not meaning any harm, he nonetheless trampled rough-shod over the sensibilities of other peoples by boasting in a loud voice about how in the States everything was bigger and better. Sometimes in Europe I have seen, and more often I have *heard*, Americans who seemed to conform to this stereotype, though they have been as often women as men, whereas in my boyhood we seem to have had no image at all of the American *woman*. (Wallis Simpson, I think, when we became aware of her in the Abdication crisis of 1936, was wholly an unknown quantity; my parents I suppose could call on no image at all, to correspond to the description, 'American *divorcée*'.) As I hope is clear, Curtis didn't in the least conform to the Harold Lloyd stereotype; he *did* mean harm, and he knew much better than to raise his voice! The only North Americans who did in some respects approximate to the model were, first, Doreen's Uncle Fred who, though long an American citizen, was Welsh-born and Welsh-bred; and, second, Herbert Marshall McLuhan, who was of course Canadian. Marshall we had met in Santa Barbara in 1958, when I would sit bemused and dazzled along with the students while Marshall gave a preliminary airing to the profoundly novel and subversive ideas that a few years later were to make of him a household word. Those later years, the years of his fame, constituted the era of the Western *gurus*, of whom Herbert Marcuse was one, and Marshall another. And Marshall, who had been in Cambridge in the 1930s, I think affected the high-wide-and-handsome Yankee – hat on back of head, camera at the ready, cigar in one extended hand – as a protective camouflage against exposure to what, in those years of the early 1960s, we were learning to call, following Marshall himself, 'the media'. I take it that from his pre-war years in England Marshall recalled the stereotype as a ready-made suit of clothes that he could put on, behind which he could hide. Since 'the media' deal in stereotypes anyway, more or less stereotyped behaviour is the best way at once to satisfy them and keep them at bay. When in those years he

Savannah, Georgia

briefly stayed with us in Cambridge, that was the explanation I found, and I was grateful. Indeed, I greatly respect Marshall for the way in which he dealt with both his sudden rise to fame, and that fame's sudden eclipse. Those of his ideas which have not been taken up (unacknowledged) into the current small change of smart talk will have to be confronted again, some day. His contention, that 'the age of print' is nearing its end, is borne out by all too many of my experiences in recent years; and if the possibility distresses me, as it does, Marshall always claimed that it distressed him too, since he was – so he always declared – himself an eager representative of that literary print culture which he found himself compelled to prognosticate the end of.

11

Puritans

I am thought to have had a long love-affair with the eighteenth century. And no wonder. Through many years I trailed my coat so that my eighteenth-century attachment should be noticed, whatever others were overlooked. To begin with, my eighteenth-century interest was as cold-blooded as that – or so it seems to me now, though on this matter as on all others memory may lie. At any rate, insofar as my eighteenth-century cloak was *not* trailed designedly, for reasons of tactics, it came into my wardrobe in the first place purely by accident. Back from the war, speedily and with good luck putting my first degree behind me, I found myself – quite improperly, I think, but from my point of view very luckily – invited to teach the courses that I had so lately and so riskily survived as a student. Among those first Cambridge students of mine was Charles Tomlinson – of whom more may be said in another place. Of the many and vast lacunae that I was aware of in my knowledge, the one that presented itself to me most pressingly was, precisely, the English eighteenth century. And so it came about that I applied myself to William Cowper and his near-contemporaries like Goldsmith when I had considerable wartime experience behind me. In that way I was much better placed to appreciate what they had to offer than I had been when, as a callow and anxious freshman before the war, I had engaged with Shakespeare and John Donne.

Neither of my chosen mentors, neither F. R. Leavis nor later Yvor Winters, had much to say about the eighteenth century. And that, I came to see, was a distinct advantage; here was a field in which I could dot the 'i's and cross the 't's of their respective judgments, could as it were amplify and extend them without, except by the remotest implication, challenging them. In this there was much dishonesty. Winters by the end of his life, following through with characteristic forthrightness an entirely reasonable objection to the epistemology of John Locke, was advancing one of the boldest and silliest of all critical verdicts – that of eighteenth-century poets in the English language the one that most deserved remembering was . . . Charles Churchill! He really meant this nonsensical judgment, as he meant every judgment that he ever pronounced. And it was less than honest in me to pretend that there was margin for civil disagreement, where in fact there wasn't. As for Leavis, his remarkably just and momentous essay on Pope was backed up by only a few (in themselves very accurate and illuminating) notes on particular poems by William Collins and Matthew Green; where one might have hoped for assessments of Cowper and Goldsmith, there was instead, in Leavis's criticism and teaching, only a vast and unargued nostalgia – for a supposed identity of purpose and concern, of cultural assumptions, between the eighteenth-century poet and his readers, a common body of assumptions and information which (so we were to think) was conspicuous by its damaging absence from all literary generations since 1800. This framework of assumptions I took over for my own, and it served me well for several years, until the course of my own reading forced me to recognize that a powerfully original poet – Christopher Smart is the obvious example – had just as much difficulty finding readers in the eighteenth century, as any poet has had in the twentieth.

In any case, as the names of Smart and Cowper and indeed Pope may suggest (to whom was added, after I got to Dublin, Berkeley), the eighteenth century was for me a religious century. And this view of it was at odds not only with the textbooks, but also with those of my own generation who shared my ardour for that hundred years. (For that, 'ardour', is what it soon became, though it had started as no more than a tactical manoeuvre.) Ian Watt and Matthew Hodgart, for example, appeared to have been drawn to the eighteenth century as to the century of 'the Enlightenment', in which secular scepticism punctured the obscurantist prejudices of the Christian churches. I stayed in touch with these friends

D.D. with grandson, 1979

of mine long enough to relish their discomfiture in the 1960s, when their irreligious 'enlightenment', renewed, turned out to have much less in common with Voltaire than with the feelingful primitivism of Rousseau.

As I write this, in November 1978, the newspapers are carrying stories about a sect called 'The People's Temple', and about a mass-suicide of several hundred devotees in a remote part of what used to be British Guiana. Faced with this and numerous other instances of what the English eighteenth century feared as 'enthusiasm', I cannot be patient with the historical scholarship that annotates 'enthusiast' and 'enthusiasm' in eighteenth-century texts, in a spirit of urbane antiquarianism, as amusing or intriguing instances of the vagaries of semantic change. If we no longer fear 'enthusiasm' as the eighteenth century did, so much the worse for us; and yet the commentators, now as in the last century, invite us to congratulate ourselves on our emancipation from that prejudice. The self-appointed seers and prophets, illumined by Inner Light which credulous thousands can be brought to believe in and trust, are all over the place in the present century. Hitler of course was one of them. And indeed they crop up more often in our political and I'm afraid our artistic life, than in religion. But such distinctions are in any case misleading, for the overwhelming of distinctions is an essential part of the strategy and the appeal of all such movements; it is of their nature to be amorphous, and therefore to have, when one comes to look, really no *doctrine* at all. Ours is an age of mish-mash, when no school of poetry can attract attention unless it can claim also to be a religion and a political programme; when no political party can succeed unless it offers its adherents the fervours and consolations of religion, and the audience-participation of the theatre; when no religious persuasion can afford not to centre itself upon 'social work'. It is undoubtedly significant, and might almost have been predicted, that one of Jim Jones's 'hitmen' should have been reared among Quakers; but my Voltairean friends, for whom the eighteenth century is the Age of Enlightenment, surely misjudge when they suppose that dangerous irrationality is peculiar to religious life. Stamp it out there, by abolishing or persecuting or emasculating the churches; and it will only crop up somewhere else – in what will look like politics or art, though it cannot seriously be either.

I was brought up in a religious milieu where, so some historians tell us, such explosions of irrationality are to be expected. I suspect that those historians are wrong: so far as I understand, any connection between the English Baptists and the tumultuously irrational Anabaptists of sixteenth-century Germany is hard to find; and on the other hand the ties between the English Baptists and their often fundamentalist and sometimes irrationalist fellow-sectaries in America were broken long ago, over the crucial issue of black slavery. However that may be, the West Riding Baptists of my childhood offended me by being tame, and altogether too cool; certainly not on the score of any irrational fervours which they might be thought to have courted or condoned. At Sheffield Road Baptist Church we had no pastors who were, or had any ambition of being, in the vocabulary of today, 'charismatic'; and I can't conceive of how we would have dealt with any minister who had that characteristic or aspired to it. In the same way, whereas Ireland is often taken to be a byword for sectarian fervour and bigotry, I cannot imagine a Christian more gently low-keyed than our Church of Ireland rector in Raheny, Tom Johnston, biographer of St Patrick. By one or another lucky chance, none of the zealots whom I have known in my life have been men of religion. Mostly they have been political, or 'politicized'. And, casting back to recover them in memory, I see disconcertingly that they all had in common one thing: the quality that we call 'charm'. Good humour was what they radiated; rough and burly in some cases, in others self-deprecating, appealingly vulnerable – but in any case they were immediately and powerfully *likeable*, and it is illegitimate wisdom after the event to say that they knew they had this quality, and traded on it. If this is what *charisma* means, or one of the guises that it may adopt, then I have experienced it, enough to take stock of it and be wary about it.

It is what F. R. Leavis had. Before now I have coupled his name with Yvor Winters's. So have others; and indeed the parallel between the two careers, on either side the Atlantic, is too marked for the comparison not to present itself. It must have some substance; and I have known many people who, drawn strongly to the one personality, could easily transfer or extend their allegiance to the other. But there is this great difference between them: Winters did not have charm, but Leavis did. People find this hard to credit, but it is true: when he wanted, and perhaps even when he didn't, Frank Leavis in person radiated a singular sweetness, and practised a civility exquisitely attuned to circumstances and to the person he was dealing with. David Levin has said of Winters, very perceptively:

> Just as the intensity of his passion must sometimes have moved his fingers over keys that expressed more anger than the occasion deserved, so his perfect ear for the language and his scorn of circumlocution must occasionally have brought reasonable indignation closer to the sound of fury.

But nothing like this could be said of Leavis. Though Leavis expressed his admiration of Doctor Johnson as critic far more vehemently and explicitly than Winters ever did, it is in Winters's critical prose, not Leavis's, that one hears the Johnsonian note. So far from scorning circumlocution,

Leavis was a master of it; and when he chooses to be brutally explicit, the brutality comes at us all the more bruisingly for emerging suddenly from a context that has been all winding and unwinding, qualification and parenthesis, allusion and innuendo. In this, one might say, Leavis was as thoroughly an English writer as Winters was an American. Winters's 'perfect ear' was for English as a written language; but Leavis's ear was for English as spoken, as spoken in England, as spoken therefore from inside some social situation that can be defined much more precisely than any American situation. And so Leavis can be, at least for a British reader, far more needling than Winters ever is. Leavis's tone is conversational, therefore intimate, almost confiding; and it is the more hurtful when our confidingness is abused. Just so have Leftist politicos abused me smilingly, addressing me by my first name, genially taking advantage of the liberal principles that they know I must hold by though they do not. Only the man like Leavis who has an unusually fine sense of civility knows how and when to drop into incivility, to most purpose. All the memoirs of D. H. Lawrence credit him with the same capacity, for warming and humanizing and refining the civilities of social intercourse precisely so that, when he wanted, he could breach them most brutally. Though I long regretted that Leavis the author of *Revaluation* had set himself up as the champion of Lawrence, I see now that it was inevitable and from his point of view right; for the Lawrence of the essays and the short stories, also of some of the poems, was indeed in his rhetorical strategies Leavis's true master.

Leavis, I suppose, would disdain using any word like 'charm'. So would Winters. And indeed the word is in bad odour, has kept too much bad company; it falls short of what I am trying to point it to – an attribute that some people have, altogether more intense and disturbing than what we usually mean by the word. Leavis at any rate had it, as clearly Lawrence had it, and as Winters didn't. And Leavis, so fearsomely all of a piece, though he wouldn't have used the name, knew very well the quality it names; and indeed, if I read him aright, got to the point where this quality – not in the least elusive, though certainly undefinable – is the pivot on which turns his entire understanding of literature, and of what literature does (or should do, or may do, or can do) in history and society. For just here and nowhere else do I locate what Leavis meant by 'life', during the many years of his later life when he maddeningly refused to acknowledge any other standard than that, for discriminating good from less good in literature. (Winters incidentally, if he had bothered to acquaint himself with what Leavis was up to, would have been outraged by this attempt to locate value in an area so nebulous – but Winters had quite enough home-grown exacerbations to nourish him, and didn't bother with British aberrations like Leavis's.) The 'life' that Leavis so doggedly looks for in literature, which towards the end he found nearly everywhere in Lawrence and in other modern authors hardly at all, can be rapidly rung through all its etymological cognates – 'vitality', 'vivacity', 'liveliness' – but ultimately comes to rest on something like 'presence', which I take to be only charm raised to a higher power. The being comprehensively and insistently *present*, on every occasion whether in literature or out of it – that was what Leavis came to esteem most highly, so highly indeed that he had little patience with any subordinate or more modest virtues; and those of us who knew him in life know that he possessed this capacity himself, supremely.

The perilousness of such a position, its kinship with the *führerprinzip*, is too manifest to be worth arguing about. What it is more difficult and therefore more instructive to acknowledge is that, in taking such a position, Leavis can draw upon common assumptions and common linguistic usage. For we have all said of such or such a one that he 'seems only half-alive', or that he 'suffers from low vitality'. (Hugh Kenner told me how Pound, responding to something disparaging said about Eliot, warned: 'Never under-estimate the Possum; he has a lot of low vitality – like a crocodile.') And of the same person or some other we may have found ourselves saying or thinking, 'His eyes are dead.' Some people are livelier than others, just as we ourselves are livelier, have more life in us, at one time than at another. To be sure the Law cannot and must not acknowledge this; it's essential to maintain the legal fiction that every life is equal to every other, and every moment of a life equal to every other moment. What Leavis and Lawrence seem to insist is that in literature that legal fiction is not to be countenanced, not ever. And then the question arises whether in making ethical and political judgments or decisions we should proceed as in a court of law, or as we quite differently proceed when composing or responding to a poem. That all men are equal anywhere but in the sight of God, is a transparent fiction; the question is whether it is a *necessary* fiction. Leavis and Lawrence seem to assert, perilously but with strong arguments, that it isn't necessary. Winters, I think, always a New Dealer, would assert that it is.

I have friends – Philip Larkin I suppose for one, Charles Sisson and Robert Conquest for others – whom I think I can hear growling: 'But what were they, anyway? Only *critics*!' I sympathize. Certainly literary criticism has got too big for its boots, and struts around too presumptuously – more foolishly in France and the United States than in Britain. But that does not apply to either Winters or Leavis, who both in fact refused to play the game by its rules and were virtually black-balled by other critics. It is they, and a very few others, who must have been in Nick Furbank's mind when he declared: 'the intellectual activity that, a hundred years ago, went into theological discussion, now finds its most natural outlet in the critical essay'. This development may be deplored – I deplore it myself, so far as it elevates the critic above the poet; but it cannot be denied. Some of the most powerful and earnest minds of our time – rather hesitantly I would elevate Lionel Trilling to parity with Leavis and Winters – have used literary criticism to advance judgments and arguments which go far beyond the judicious assessment of works of literature. And surely Furbank is right: the energy that we detect in Winters and Leavis, in Trilling also, is an energy that we think of as 'theological'.

This has been widely acknowledged: 'puritanical' is the word that has been used of both Winters and Leavis, just as 'rabbinical' is the stone that has been cast at Trilling. 'Puritan' is a tag that has been tied to me also; which delights me, because I deliberately courted it, and because the import of it is, however grudgingly, complimentary. If 'charm' is one word that we have cheapened and loosened to the point where we cannot self-respectingly use it except inside quotation-marks, 'puritan' and 'puritanical' are words already far down the same slippery slide. By a 'puritan' nowadays we mean what an earlier generation would have called a 'person of principle'. Let the principles avowed be as far from those of historical puritanism as D. H. Lawrence's were, still 'puritan' is what we call him simply because principles is what he had and held by – not all moral and intellectual judgments were, for him, *relative*.

All the same, we can't for ever postpone acknowledging that Leavis and Winters, and Lawrence too, specifically refused their assent to that body of beliefs which historically all puritans, along with other Christians, have adhered to. Through most of the years when I hearkened to these men, I was in the same spiritual twilight: hung up, and with no great anxiety either, between Belief and Unbelief. I'm not particularly ashamed of that, though I dare say I ought to be. But I think it has to be the case that such crepuscular uncertainty about First and Last Things disperses itself, like a miasma, through the crevices of thought about apparently quite other things, accustoming us to approximations merely, and twilight zones in our thinking, about such entirely secular matters as the proper language for poetry. If the honest agnostic protests to me, 'What can I do about it?' I have little answer to give, and certainly no narrative of a surprising conversion such as might stir the deluded followers of the Reverend Jim Jones, or the snake-handlers of East Tennessee. That such instantaneous and spectacular conversions do occur, I firmly believe; and to account for them with talk of mass-hysteria is merely and gratuitously to prefer one model of what 'explanation' is, to John Wesley's alternative explanation that when God intervenes in history, we can expect to find laws suspended, norms defied, and our normal expectations reversed or outraged. But in my case the change was unspectacular, gradual and (so I am tempted to say, but wrongly) imperceptible. If I were to pinpoint a crux, it would be when I learned from my mentor, the Reverend Harold Brumbaum of Los Altos, California, that what matters is the physical act of worship, not the mental act of belief or assent. Thus, 'Try it, and see' is the only honest answer I can give.

Few of my friends at the present day or at any time in the past, whether they are Christians like Harold Brumbaum or free-thinkers like Ian Watt, share or can understand the sympathy that I have for puritans like Winters and Leavis. And indeed, so far as 'puritan' equals 'zealot', I understand their squeamishness. Much more to the taste of my Christian friends, among whom I include my son and daughter-in-law, is the serenely Catholic temper of a C. S. Lewis or even a J. R. R. Tolkien. And it is surely true that the personality of Lewis, and the record of Lewis's life, provide more comforting and admirable spectacles. Moreover I stand ready to condemn the political and ideological zealot, whenever I detect him; and it is also true that when I turn to a page of Leavis's or Winters's writings, I often recoil from the brutality of their tone. In truth there is only one area in which I endorse the zealot, and am grateful for him; but that is the area where I have most invested – the area where I figure in my own mind not as intellectual but as artist. Nowhere but in the arts are the battle-lines drawn so tautly as the zealots pretend, nowhere else is there ultimately no room for compromise, for face-saving formulae, for 'Live, and let live'. That I often cannot concur in either Leavis's or Winters's way of dividing the sheep from the goats, is beside the point: what I esteem in both of them is their common insistence that sheep there are, and goats there are; that in the arts, as between the genuine and the fake, or between the achieved and the unachieved, there cannot be any halfway house. The Calvinist doctrines of election and reprobation may be false and brutal in every other realm of human endeavour; in the arts they rule. And the catholicism of Lewis and Tolkien becomes, when extended into the arts, merely a lax eclecticism; worse, it becomes – because of its tenderness towards 'the ordinary' – indistinguishable, in its impact on the practising artist, from that secular social democracy which from every other point of view is its enemy. Between the artist and the philistine (of whatever class) there is war to the death; and only zealots like Leavis and Winters have proclaimed that unpalatable truth, in season and out of season. It is because Lionel Trilling's grasp of this truth is less firm than Leavis's or Winters's, that I hesitate about admitting him to their company.

The case that of recent years most brought this home to me was that of my friend, the late Howard Warshaw. And it came home to me with the more force because Howard was himself no puritan at all, in his domestic and social life, but on the contrary genial, gregarious, relaxed. I had met Howard, painter and teacher of painting, when we were first in California, in 1957–8. One Sunday morning in that year, Howard, a black-avised bull of a man, hurled at me and my twelve-year-old Mark a baseball or else an ovoid football (I don't now remember which) on behalf of himself and his twelve-year-old stepson, another Mark. This was in Hope Ranch, an affluent rural suburb of Santa Barbara where on weekdays, having delivered my Mark to his private school, I would bemusedly stop my car to watch the plumes of water from behind the Sierra Nevada bow and curtsey in distant silence, watering opulent lawns. What I didn't know then, nor was to learn until twenty years later, what Howard himself didn't know, was that the high point of his career in terms of public acceptance, the historical moment at which his kind of painting might have won recognition, was already past. Strenuously abstracted though they were, Howard's canvases – and his *walls*, for he was very actively and seriously a painter of murals – were ultimately 'figurative'. He painted, by principle, *from nature*; for he believed, as I heard him declare confidently and with eloquence on many occasions, that painting was a way of analysing the natural world that confronts us – a way of knowing that world, analytically. In this, so far as I can see, he was at one with John Constable and, as he would over the years contend ever more vehemently, with Tintoretto. But no sooner had he left his native New York than the non-figurative dogmas of Abstract Expressionism monopolized the entire art-world, and canvases painted on those principles began to command sums such as, I am glad to say, could not be approached by even the most publicized achievements of my own art of poetry. Over twenty years I came to see – only gradually, for Howard had too much self-respect to wear his heart on his sleeve – how damning to an earnest artist, not just in terms of worldly success but because of what it does to his self-esteem, can be the fluctuations of philistine but sophisticated fashion, especially when many thousands of dollars are invested in what is at any given time *à la mode*. Howard was temperamentally quite averse to the puritan's bleak alternatives of all-or-nothing; yet by the end he could not explain what had happened to his life as an artist except in those non-negotiable terms.

Howard, I suppose, may be called an irreligious man. His father, who survived him, was a non-practising Jew, and so far as I know always had been. Howard himself declared: 'I have too much respect for the natural to believe in the supernatural, but I do believe in the superhuman.' And it is that belief – in the superhuman – which makes 'irreligious' seem the wrong word for him, almost as wrong as 'puritan' or 'puritanical'. The muscular turbulence of his work, as I experience it, tempts me to associate with his own word, 'superhuman', the word 'baroque'. But I may be illegitimately importing this idea from what I know of the work and personality of his master, Rico Lebrun. At any rate a big man, a bear or a bull; muscularity was his distinguishing feature, in his physical presence and his intellectual life, as well as his art. In the polemical testament which he tried to compose in a rush in the last months of his life, as in the polemic which I composed on his behalf to show to him before he died, there is unavoidably a shrillness and stridency, the hectoring and driving note of the purist or the puritan; and in this there is a sort of betrayal of the largeness and magnanimity of the man, of how happily he inhabited his massive frame, and how gratefully (though fastidiously also) he enjoyed his sheer physical being. I must some day get into print this polemic of mine, not simply so as to close my accounts with him, and not only because it says things important to me, but so as to recover for myself – when that unfinished business is thus finished – the merry good companion and family man, Howard the burly and elegant polo-player, scooting in his jeep down Toro Canyon, between the avocado groves, into the shoreline overcast of Carpinteria.

It was, pitifully, sudden and massive surgery for stomach-cancer that set Howard to writing his one and only book, soon to appear, *Drawings on Drawing*. He was barely convalescent before he called for his drawing-board and began writing it, propped up in his bed, using the draftsman's fat fountain-pen that was seldom out of his hands. As soon as he was out of hospital he sent for me to come down and help him with the writing; and I flew down from Northern California, to be met by him, a stooped and shrunken figure, at the Santa Barbara airport. That must have been in 1976, in the early summer before I left for England, spending perhaps three nights in Howard's and Franny's guest-house, with its sun-deck above the avocado trees. Recognizing accurately that the surgeon had won him a reprieve that could not last for long, Howard was in a fever to find a publisher. But the book, quite apart from being unpolished and in fact unfinished, was necessarily an awkward and expensive one, for it was to be not a manifesto but a *demonstration*, and so the heart of it had to be 24 plates of drawings by Howard. The only possible publisher was the one whom Howard had claims on through his years of teaching on the Santa Barbara campus, the University of California Press. And when that chance fell through, by a series of mischances, I knew that no other major publisher would accept it so promptly as Howard quite desperately wanted; so I deceived him, going through the motions of hawking the idea of the book to publishing houses in London as well as New York, simply to keep his spirits up right to the end. Part of that deception was the introductory essay that I wrote, which Howard liked so much that he began talking of the book as a work of collaboration, in which my name would figure with his on the title-page. His touching misjudgment on this point, as on others, recalled to me the drug-dimmed miscalculations years before of Douglas Brown, whom in his last weeks I had compassionately deceived in a similar way. And in any case my piece was in most ways not a deception at all: it truthfully reconsidered my art through the glass of his, and it truthfully made common cause with him, so that his ardent welcome of it is not anything that I need feel guilty about. I should have been prepared for what happened, and certainly I wasn't wounded by it: when Howard was dead, and the responsibility for bringing out *Drawings on Drawing* devolved upon a young kinsman with the help and advice of some of Howard's ex-pupils, my Introduction was thought too intransigent and uncompromising, too strident I suppose, in a word too *puritan*. Who knows? Perhaps those young men are wise in their generation. Still, it was a statement that Howard Warshaw approved; and since I still stand over it myself, I will one way or another publish it.

Ah yes, but Howard and Franny had figured in my life – in *our* life, Doreen's and mine – far more largely than this artificially isolated crux can suggest. Howard had known Igor and Vera Stravinsky, and through them the whole community of Europe's intellectual and artistic *émigrés* who found haven in Los Angeles. He knew, though I did not, Christopher Isherwood. It was he and I, along with others like Douwe Stuurman and Elmer Noble, who in 1958 steered the exquisitely courteous and already almost blind Aldous Huxley to a seat in a Santa Barbara restaurant; and it was Howard who, after I had returned to Europe, shepherded Huxley through his stay in Santa Barbara and is named in Sybille Bedford's biography of Huxley. It was Howard and Franny who in the 1970s, when the Southern Pacific's passenger service (which I had delighted in) had been replaced by the dubiously contrived AMTRAK, brought to San Jose railroad station our common friends George and Mary-Lou Dangerfield, there, the four of them, to be met by me and my younger son, and whirled away to our house in Stanford. On that visit Howard, already ill, happily played second fiddle to 'Geo' who was studying Anglo-Irish relations and so must be brought to meet Conor Cruise O'Brien and his wife, Maire, whom we knew – Conor, at any rate – from our Dublin days. Years before, an idle Cambridge undergraduate had earned from me an alpha on at least one Tripos paper by showing he had read and assimilated Geo's *Strange Death of Liberal England*. This, I dare say, is name-dropping, such as I have rather carefully abjured on earlier pages of these reminiscences; if I indulge it now, it is to acknowledge that from Howard I learned, after much initial distrust had been broken down, how knowing the most distinguished people in a given milieu may derive not from any toadying alertness but from having a sure nose for human distinction, and homing in on it with as much to give as to receive.

Afterword, for my wife

Because I am unobservant – only now do I observe that our ivory Ganesh has been on display to guests for months, though a week ago I looked for it in vain, to elucidate an allusion – am I therefore insensitive? It seems you do not think so, for you appeal to me on questions of symmetry and asymmetry, and I notice you quite often fall in with my suggestions.

And can I be thought insensitive to *sound* when on the contrary I pick up and inveigh against all sorts of background *noise*, comprehending in that unflattering category even Beethoven?

By using a faculty only infrequently – seldom do I really and consciously *see*, seldom thus *hear* – may one not keep that faculty innocently sharp and keen, whereas habitual use would have dulled it? Such education as there is, in aesthetic perception, proceeds on the opposite assumption – that nice and right judgment is the result of continual practice, of optical or auricular alertness made constant and habitual. But may it not be that we properly cherish the capacities brought to us through eye and ear, only when we *husband* those resources – by most of the time *not* seeing, *not* hearing? You will laugh at such special pleading.

In the past you have not laughed, but expostulated: 'You a poet, and you notice so little!' What I notice is words, and the sounded or unsounded cadences that words make when they are strung together; names, not the things they name. Useless for me to regret this, or for you to reproach me with it. And sure enough, you stopped reproaching me long ago. But this fact that we both know seems unknown to most of those who talk or write about literature. F. R. Leavis used to distinguish between a feeling *for* words, and a feeling *with* them or *through* them. And this makes sense; in particular it diagnoses and impales one sort of dishonest writing – the fine, the purple passage, orotund, informed with a feeling for words that in fact is *un*feeling, mere glacial connoisseurship. But it is too brutal all the same, this dichotomy; it makes a reader like Leavis too distrustful of writers like Conrad, or Faulkner, or Yeats, who flirt with purple passages, and from time to time perpetrate them. Hard, with such writers, and sometimes impossible, to tell the purple from the true blue.

Somewhere, in books I have not read, a speculative psychologist or epistemologist must have wondered if it is possible in fact to name a name, without somehow conjuring up at least the phantom of that which

175

is named. And such phantasmal acquaintance as we thus get with the actual world, though without doubt it is inadequate for many purposes, and dangerously so – may it not be for literature, for *poetry*, not just adequate but indispensable, irreplaceable, precisely the sort of traffic with the actual that literature lives by, and exists to promote? Does it not, precisely by being so hazy, permit of symmetrical or asymmetrical arrangements (shapes, that is, and forms) such as the conscientious naturalist not only cannot command, but must not aim at? (Gilbert White of Selborne is a charmer; but is he, in any but the most literal sense, a *writer?*)

More special pleading, you see. But at the end of a venture like this, modest though it is, being conscious of so much left out – lepers in Ceylon, mutilated professional beggars beside a 1940s train in Madras, variously frenzied people known in Essex in the 1960s – how can the writer enter any plea that is *not* 'special', quite specially pleading for indulgence?

And from no one more than you? Of course!